A YEAR OF BIRDS

Foreword by Peter Alden

A YEAR *of* BIRDS

Writings on Birds from the Journal of HENRY DAVID THOREAU

Edited by
Geoff Wisner

Illustrated by
Barry Van Dusen

MUP/ P687

Published by Mercer University Press
1501 Mercer University Drive
Macon, Georgia 31207

28 27 26 25 24   5 4 3 2 1

Books published by Mercer University Press are printed on acid-free
paper that meets the requirements of the American National Standard for
Information Sciences—Permanence of Paper for Printed Library Materials.

Printed and bound in Canada.

This book is set in Minion Pro, Felix Titling, and Meta Pro.
Book design by Burt&Burt.

ISBN 978-0-88146-917-2

Cataloging-in-Publication Data is available from the Library of Congress

A YEAR OF BIRDS

FOREWORD

BY PETER ALDEN

Admiration for Henry Thoreau has stood the test of time. He had so much to observe, think about, and write—about society, his friends and townsfolk, politics, science, literature, slavery, Native Americans, making a living, and the natural world.

Henry Thoreau was born in and mostly lived in his beloved Concord, Massachusetts, about twenty miles northwest of Boston and Cambridge. Axes, saws, and fires had transformed the once heavily forested landscape into a vast farmscape of crops, orchards, and grassland for livestock, with remnant woodland.

While millions have read *Walden*, many fewer have read even part of Henry's enormous Journal. For his whole adult life, he followed the seasons and made observations on plants, insects, fish, reptiles, amphibians, mammals, and birds (among many other subjects). Although that work has not been as popular as *Walden*, it has spawned all sorts of books, journal articles, and discussion over the years.

Most of Henry's careful observations were focused on plants and birds. Virtually every day he wrote about various birds that he saw, heard, or were reported to him. From his records we can compare the arrival times of the summertime birds in his day with their arrival times today. We can also clearly see how bird populations have changed, with the loss of most grassland birds, the northward retreat of birds from the boreal forest, and the increase in southern birds.

I can't claim to be the world's most knowledgeable ornithologist or most accomplished Thoreau scholar, but I stay in touch with, and "bird" with, several dozen local bird experts. I was born in Concord's

Emerson Hospital in early July in the mid-1940s. The hospital overlooks the Sudbury River, with Walden Woods beyond. My family lived on Main Street in Concord near the Assabet River, where Henry paddled frequently. When I was a kid, my brothers and I would explore the riverside woods and meadows. My first school was the Thoreau School. I learned how to swim at Walden Pond.

My father was an amateur birder with lousy opera glasses that we kids would fight to borrow when he wanted us to see a heron or an oriole while on a walk, a canoe trip, or climbing a mountain in New Hampshire. My mother would read to me from *The Burgess Bird Book for Children*, which had great color paintings by Louis Agassiz Fuertes. We also had a big Fuertes art book called *Portraits of New England Birds* that showed birds in their correct habitat.

I wanted to see those birds, but I didn't have binoculars for several years. That forced me to climb a huge Norway spruce in our backyard to see some warblers. I wasn't interested in hunting birds—neither of my parents were hunters, and they had a general dislike of guns—and I never got heavily into finding bird nests, as I was admonished that if you approached a nest or touched the eggs, the nest might be abandoned.

Once I shoveled enough snow and mowed enough lawns, I was finally able to buy some decent binoculars and a Peterson Field Guide. I got around by bicycle, sometimes with fellow kid birders such as my brother David and our friends Bob and Eddie Woodin. We went to many of Henry's places, from Walden Pond to Great Meadows to the Estabrook Woods and the Sudbury and Wayland marshlands. I kept a journal of all those early trips and the birds we saw.

How many towns had their own bird book? Fortunately, ours did. In 1949, Harvard University Press published *Birds of Concord* by Ludlow Griscom. I had a copy. It had lengthy discussions of changing habitats and bird life over time, with many references to where and when Henry noted various birds. I would bicycle to those places and search for birds of interest and eventually I started leading bird walks at Great Meadows for Boston bird clubs.

My high school, Concord-Carlisle, is located in a corner of Walden Woods not far from Walden Pond. Our cross-country trail is now part of the Emerson-Thoreau Ramble. While I played on the football and basketball teams, I irritated our baseball coach by not trying out for the baseball team. I needed spring afternoons to walk with Henry's ghost and welcome back our birds.

By the time I graduated, I had seen most of New England's birds. I wasn't fond of New England winters, so I took off for the University of Arizona. I joined the Tucson Audubon Society and was elected vice president for the next four years. Sonoita Creek and Patagonia Lake were about an hour's drive south of the university, and I championed the effort to save the stream and its woodlands, which became the Nature Conservancy's Patagonia-Sonoita Creek Preserve.

The Pacific coast of Mexico beckoned. I would often take long weekends, riding the Nogales-Mazatlán-Guadalajara train and getting off at various stops along the coast with a sleeping bag, water, and Campbell's soup, which I would eat unheated from the can. While still enrolled in college, I led three or four two-week trips all over Mexico, and I got away with it. When I graduated, young men were being drafted for Vietnam, but the army decided I was 4-F due to shoulder injuries I got playing football. I spent most of the next year traveling and birding around the world, from Europe to Southern Asia, New Guinea, Australia, New Zealand, and many Pacific islands.

Over the next few years, I led dozens of successful and pioneering birding tours to Mexico, Central and South America, Portugal, and Spain. As a result, I was invited to create a worldwide bird and nature tour program for a major environmental organization. Which one? The Massachusetts Audubon Society, whose headquarters were in Lincoln, about a mile east of Walden Pond. I moved to Cambridge and began leading bird and nature tours to six continents every year. Eventually, I was hired by Lindblad Travel, the Harvard Museum of Natural History, Overseas Adventure Travel, Thomson Safaris, Road Scholar, and many cruise lines to lead trips in a hundred countries and lecture about birds and nature.

In the 1990s, I moved from Cambridge back to my hometown of Concord and began attending the Annual Gathering of the Thoreau Society, leading nature walks and giving a few lectures. I also began writing a series of field guides, including the *National Audubon Society Field Guide to New England*, which included more than a thousand plants and animals. Over time, these guides have sold more than three million copies, helping turn many people into local naturalists.

Back in 1960, when I was still in high school, I organized Concord's very first Christmas bird count, an Audubon Society tradition that dated back to 1900. But when I began producing field guides for Audubon, I had an epiphany: Why just count birds? And why only in the dead of winter?

On July 4, 1998, Professor Edward O. Wilson of Harvard and I gathered hundreds of expert field biologists to run the world's first serious bioblitz. The date was chosen to honor the anniversary of the day Henry moved into his cabin at Walden Pond. In one day, within five miles of Walden Pond, we found nearly two thousand species of plants, fungi, lichens, mammals, reptiles, amphibians, fishes, invertebrates—and exactly one hundred species of birds.

The Walden Woods Project, National Geographic, and the National Park Service sponsored similar major bioblitzes centered at Walden in 2009 and 2019, with more than 3,600 species certified by experts and/or community members of the online resource iNaturalist. Bioblitzes now take place in dozens of states and countries.

How many of those birds would Henry have seen? And how many did he see that are gone today?

Before game laws, sanctuaries, or wildlife refuges, people in Henry's day could shoot any sort of wildlife: for food, as "vermin," or for target practice. As a result, he never saw ravens, turkey vultures, or wild turkeys. But of the birds he chronicled, the passenger pigeon is the only species to become extinct.

Of the other forest birds, whippoorwills have vanished from Concord due to a huge decline in the large moths they feed on. Olive-sided flycatchers, least flycatchers, and purple finches no longer breed in our area, having retreated to cooler areas to the north. Three thrushes whose songs Henry loved—the veery, wood thrush, and hermit thrush—have become rather rare. Acid rain has killed the calcium-rich land snails these thrushes need in their diet to lay eggs with sturdy shells.

Native shrublands and sunny second-growth woodlands are now scarce in Concord. We have lost all our ruffed grouse, which Henry called partridges. Colorful warblers such as the chestnut-sided, golden-winged, Nashville, and prairie warbler no longer breed here. Brown thrashers and towhees, once widespread, are barely hanging on.

In the mid-1800s, 90 percent of New England south of the White Mountains was a vast sea of grassland, created by man for grazing cows, horses, and sheep. The commonest birds in Concord were those adapted to the prairie that had moved east when the forests were cut: upland sandpipers, meadowlarks, bobolinks, and open-country sparrows such as the field, grasshopper, and vesper sparrow. All these are now gone, or extremely scarce. Nighthawks no longer breed here, as overuse of pesticides has caused a massive decline in large aerial insects.

The marshes of Concord are less extensive due to the regrowth of red maples and other plants. Chemical pollution and the spread of invasive plants, such as American lotus, phragmites, purple loosestrife, and water chestnut, have adversely affected marsh-nesting birds. Black ducks, northern harriers, Wilson's snipe, pied-billed grebes, and both American bitterns and least bitterns have declined or vanished as breeders.

Some birds unknown to Henry, at least in Concord, have become much more common. The Canada goose, which Henry noted only as a nervous migrant, now lives here year-round. Geese are now the commonest bird in our winter bird count. Huge mute swans can be seen on most of our ponds and rivers (but not the deep waters of Walden Pond). Mallards, a Great Plains breeder that Henry never saw, have vanquished our black ducks. Rock pigeons nest in highway overpasses, and house sparrows and starlings crowd birdfeeders and evict native bluebirds and tree swallows from our birdhouses.

Various southern birds have migrated north since Henry's day and can now be seen in Concord. These include Carolina wrens, northern cardinals, northern mockingbirds, red-bellied woodpeckers, and tufted titmice. Most have inched northward not because of climate change but because of the explosion in the number of birdfeeders and invasive plant fruits. (The northern migration of the blue-gray gnatcatcher, unknown to Henry, is due to climate change.) Mourning doves also remain in huge numbers through the winter rather than migrating to the southern states.

Finally, some of the birds Henry observed only rarely can now be seen in greater numbers. Bald eagles and ospreys nest in Concord, and Cooper's hawks and red-tailed hawks are common year-round. Great egrets and snowy egrets visit regularly in the warmer months. The return of beavers has resulted in swamps where tall dead trees stand in water deep enough to deter predators, making them a safe home for great blue heron nests. Wood ducks and hooded mergansers are much more common, encouraged by wood duck boxes and riverside trees with nesting cavities. Henry never saw the huge pileated woodpecker in Concord (he did see one in Maine), while today we likely have two dozen nesting pairs in town.

In recent years, and especially with the pandemic killing most cruises and safaris, I have had the privilege of working part time at the Thoreau

Society Shop at Walden Pond. I look out at the pond with Henry's cabin nearby. I meet Thoreauvians, many naturalists, and folks from all over the world. Most have heard of the man who lived deliberately, lived in the woods, and was a light in the darkness. Few of these visitors are aware of his serious fascination with the life of birds. I trust that Geoff Wisner's careful selection of Henry's bird notes for every day of the year, along with the stunning art work of my friend Barry Van Dusen, will inspire you to saunter in your local wild places with binoculars and a field guide.

PREFACE

When Houghton Mifflin published Thoreau's Journal in 1906, it chose Bradford Torrey, an ornithologist, to be its editor. Torrey, it turned out, was less than generous in his appraisal of Thoreau as a birder. After noting that Thoreau didn't buy a "glass"—a brass and mahogany spyglass—until 1854, he goes on,

> But glass or no glass, how could an ornithological observer, whose power—so Emerson said—"seemed to indicate additional senses," be in the field daily for ten or fifteen years before setting eyes upon his first rose-breasted grosbeak?—which memorable event happened to Thoreau on the 13th of June, 1853! How could a man who had made it his business for at least a dozen years to "name all the birds without a gun," stand for a long time within a few feet of a large bird, so busy that it could not be scared far away, and then go home uncertain whether he had been looking at a woodcock or a snipe? How could he, when thirty-five years old, see a flock of sparrows, and hear them sing, and not be sure whether or not they were chipping sparrows? And how could a man so strong in times and seasons, always marking dates with an almanac's exactness, how could he, so late as '52, inquire concerning the downy woodpecker, one of the more familiar and constant of year-round birds, "Do we see him in the winter?"

Four years later, Francis H. Allen, Torrey's uncredited coeditor, mined the Journal to create *Notes on New England Birds*. In his preface, Allen states that Thoreau "never acquired much skill in the diagnosis of birds seen in the field." He admits, however, that "Thoreau seems to have *seen* things pretty accurately." In Allen's estimation, "His chief difficulty in identification was, perhaps, a tendency to jump at conclusions,—as when, meeting with the pileated woodpecker in the Maine woods, he at once set it down as the 'red-headed woodpecker (*Picus erythrocephalus*),' evidently because of its conspicuous red crest."

Half a century later, in 1964, Helen Cruickshank published *Thoreau on Birds*, which included writings on birds from *Walden*, *Cape Cod*, *The Maine Woods*, and his final journey to Minnesota, as well as a discussion of the ornithological guides available to him: John James Audubon, Thomas Nuttall, Alexander Wilson, and others.

Cruickshank is more generous than her predecessors in her assessment of Thoreau's birding skills.

> The fact that Thoreau frequently applied the blanket term "wood thrush" to all thrushes has been repeated through the years by his casual readers as evidence that he could not distinguish between the species. Entries in the Journal belie this. On occasion he placed notes in his Journal that prove he was able to identify the Wood Thrush, the Hermit Thrush, and the Veery if the situation permitted him to study the bird with care. He had trouble with sparrows, but bird watchers today, using the best binoculars and the finest field guide, experience difficulties and uncertainty at times in the field identification of sparrows in immature plumages or when a brief glimpse of the bird is possible. Hawks and "beach-birds" also presented Thoreau with puzzles. But he continued to study each new bird with care, note its colors as precisely as possible, assign a name to it, and then reexamine his reference books in the light of his newest observations. Repeatedly he rechecked his own notes for accuracy.

In his short and somewhat perfunctory foreword to Cruickshank's book, Roger Tory Peterson echoes others when he says, "It may be argued that the hermit of Concord made no great contribution to the science of ornithology," but notes that Thoreau was "the first of a long succession of observers to make notes on the avian residents and visitors of the Concord River Valley." More to the point, he writes that "although Thoreau's interest in birds may not have been particularly scientific, his writings about them have had more than ordinary influence, for he saw them through the eyes of a philosopher."

Francis Allen may have put it best when he wrote of Thoreau, "He never became in any respect an expert ornithologist, and some of the reasons are not far to seek. He was too intent on becoming an expert analogist, for one thing. It better suited his genius to trace some analogy between the soaring hawk and his own thoughts than to make a scientific study of the bird."

As Allen might have predicted, the importance of Thoreau's bird writings to readers today is more literary than scientific. Certainly many of the most memorable things he wrote about birds have nothing to do with exact description.

"The bluebird carries the sky on its back."

"The quail—invisible—whistles, and who attends."

Unlike earlier collections, but along the lines of my previous collections of Thoreau's writings on animals and wildflowers, *A Year of Birds* is organized not by the type of bird—warbler, raptor, thrush, and so on—but by the day of the year. The entries all come from the Journal, and they all record observations in and around Concord, Massachusetts.

The importance of the seasons to Thoreau's sense of nature and spirit is almost impossible to overstate. By presenting his birds chronologically, we can see when different birds appeared at the same time, when the same bird appeared at different seasons, and what that meant to Thoreau's spiritual and emotional life.

A Year of Birds includes birds inexplicably left out by other editors, such as the Blackburnian warbler, as well as thoughts about birds in general not included in previous collections. It includes hunting stories and descriptions of skinning and mounting birds, birds in museums, and birds as metaphor.

Special sections are devoted to the passenger pigeon and to Thoreau's "night warbler." Thoreau describes passenger pigeons as "fabulous birds with their long tails and their pointed breasts" and reports how in Concord they were baited with pounded acorns, then netted and sold for food. The night warbler was a mystery to Thoreau, who spent years trying to match a distinctive song with the bird that made it. Was it a white-eyed vireo? A Nashville warbler? A white-throated sparrow? A common yellowthroat? Or was it (at least most of the time) an ovenbird? (Thoreau's similar confusion over the identity of the "seringo bird" was the result of his difficulty telling the various sparrows apart.)

Unlike earlier collections, *A Year of Birds* offers a wealth of color illustrations: one hundred fifty drawings and watercolors by award-winning artist Barry Van Dusen. Based in Massachusetts, Barry has spent years observing and drawing birds and other wildlife in the field. Many of the illustrations used in *A Year of Birds* come from his field sketchbooks. Their freshness and spontaneity perfectly complement the descriptions in Thoreau's Journal, the great work that Thoreau once commented could have been titled "Field Notes."

ACKNOWLEDGMENTS

Several years ago, at an Annual Gathering of the Thoreau Society, Tom Potter, a past president of the society, buttonholed me and insisted that I should edit a collection of Thoreau's writings on birds.

"It would fly off the shelves!" he said.

I have never been sure how much of this advice was sincere and how much was said for the sake of the pun, but I'm grateful to Tom for prompting me to think about how I could present Thoreau's thoughts on birds in a way that hasn't been done before.

I was pleased and honored that Peter Alden agreed once again to verify the various species of birds in this book—which often meant checking Thoreau's own identifications. With the help of his fellow Concord birder Simon Perkins, he has saved me, and perhaps Henry, from a few embarrassing blunders. This time around I was also able to persuade him to write a foreword, and in this way I have learned more than I knew about his life with birds, especially the birds of Concord.

Peter's friend and fellow Massachusetts birder Barry Van Dusen made possible what may be the best feature of this book: dozens of drawings and watercolors of Thoreau's birds, created in the field over the course of decades. Just as Thoreau once wrote that he had never gotten over his surprise at having been born in Concord, "the most estimable place in all the world," I have not yet gotten over my surprise and delight that, when I approached him to illustrate this book, it turned out that Barry had already observed and painted nearly every bird it contains.

For support both general and specific, I would like to thank my old friends Chris Carduff and Bill Schwartz. Chris's untimely death in 2023 is a loss that I and many others will feel for a long time to come.

I also thank a list of Thoreauvians and nature lovers that includes Gail Addiss, Ray Angelo, Michael Berger, Kristen Case, Ken Chaya, Phyllis Cole, Cherrie Corey, Jeff Cramer, Victor Curran, Ted David, Allan DiBiase, John Eiche, Jill Erickson, James Finley, Mike Frederick, Mark Gallagher, Jayne Gordon, Rebecca Gould, Bob Gross, Danny Heitman, Rich Higgins, Ron Hoag, Christoph Irmscher, D. B. Johnson, Rochelle Johnson, Christina Katopodis, Lawrence Klaes, John Kucich, Elise Lemire, Michael Lorence, Deborah Medenbach, Dennis Noson, Michiko Ono, Henrik Otterberg, Audrey Raden, Brent Ranalli, Tamara Rose, Paul Schacht, Bill Schechter, Michael Schleifer, Corinne H. Smith, Richard Smith, François Specq, Catherine Staples, Bergur Thorgeirsson, Robert Thorson, Jeff VanderMeer, Laura Dassow Walls, Gabriel Willow, and Elizabeth Witherell.

And as always, my thanks to Jenn for her love, patience, and support.

A NOTE ON THE TEXT

As in my previous collections of excerpts from Thoreau's Journal, I have begun with the 1906 edition of the Journal edited by Bradford Torrey and Francis H. Allen, then checked the selected passages against the eight published volumes of the Princeton University Press edition and the editors' transcripts for the portion of the Journal not yet published by Princeton (September 3, 1854, to November 3, 1861).

I have restored much of Thoreau's punctuation, especially his dashes, and eliminated many of the commas, hyphens, and semicolons added by Torrey and Allen. I have restored sentence fragments and paragraph breaks as Thoreau originally wrote them.

Thoreau's spelling and punctuation were often inconsistent. For instance, he sometimes wrote "hen-hawk" and sometimes "hen hawk," sometimes "grey" and other times "gray." (Thoreau's hen hawk was usually a red-tailed hawk, sometimes a red-shouldered hawk.) When necessary, I chose the version that was less punctuated, more American, and closer to modern usage. While Thoreau referred to the note of the chickadee as *phebe* or *phoebe*, I have used *phebe* throughout to reduce confusion with the eastern phoebe, which he sometimes mistakenly called a pewee.

Where Thoreau quotes from William Wood's 1634 book *New England's Prospect* (January 24, 1855), I have followed Wood's original spelling and punctuation rather than Thoreau's approximate transcription.

A YEAR OF BIRDS

MARCH

March 1, 1855

I hear several times the fine drawn *phe-be* note of the chickadee—which I heard only once during the winter. Singular that I should hear this on the first spring day. . . .

Goodwin says that somewhere where he lived they called cherry birds [cedar waxwings] "port-royals."

March 2, 1859

The bluebird, which some woodchopper or inspired walker is said to have seen in that sunny interval between the snowstorms, is like a speck of clear blue sky seen near the end of a storm reminding us of an ethereal region and a heaven which we had forgotten. Princes and magistrates

Eastern bluebird

are often styled serene—but what is their turbid serenity to that ethereal serenity which the bluebird embodies? His most serene Birdship! His soft warble melts in the ear, as the snow is melting in the valleys—around. The bluebird comes and with his warble drills the ice—and sets free the rivers and ponds and frozen ground. As the sand flows down the slopes a little way assuming the forms of foliage where the frost comes out of the ground so this little rill of melody flows a short way down the concourse of the sky.

March 3, 1859

Going by the solidago oak at Clamshell Hill bank, I heard a faint rippling note and looking up saw about fifteen snow buntings sitting in the top of the oak all with their breasts toward me—sitting so still and quite white seen against the white cloudy sky. They did not look like birds—but the ghosts of birds—and their boldness, allowing me to come quite near, enhanced this impression. They were almost as white as snowballs, and from time to time I heard a low soft rippling note from them. I could see no features—but only the general outline of plump birds in white. It was a very spectral sight, and after I had watched them for several minutes I can hardly say that I was prepared to see them fly away like ordinary buntings when I advanced further. At first they were almost concealed by being almost the same color with the cloudy sky.

March 4, 1840

I learned today that my ornithology had done me no service. The birds I heard, which fortunately did not come within the scope of my science, sung as freshly as if it had been the first morning of creation, and had for background to their song an untrodden wilderness—stretching through many a Carolina and Mexico of the soul.

March 5, 1860

The song sparrows begin to sing *hereabouts*.

I see some tame ducks in the river—six of them. It is amusing to see how exactly perpendicular they will stand with their heads on the bottom and their tails up—plucking some food there—three or four at once. Perhaps the grass etc. is a little further advanced there for them.

Snow buntings in flight

March 6, 1858

I see the first hen hawk, or hawk of any kind methinks since the beginning of winter. Its scream even is inspiring as the voice of a spring bird.

March 7, 1859

I come out to hear a spring bird—the ground generally covered with snow yet and the channel of the river only partly open. On the Hill I hear first the tapping of a small woodpecker. I then see a bird alight on the dead top of the highest white oak on the hilltop—on the topmost point. It is a shrike. While I am watching him eight or ten rods off—I hear robins down below west of the hill. Then, to my surprise the shrike begins to sing. It is at first a wholly ineffectual and inarticulate sound—without any solid tone to it—a mere hoarse breathing as if he were clearing his throat—unlike any bird that I know, a shrill hissing. Then he uttered a kind of mew, a very decided mewing clear and wiry between that of a catbird and the note of the nuthatch. As if to lure a nuthatch within his reach. Then rose with the sharpest shrillest vibratory or tremulous whistling or chirruping on the very highest key. This high gurgling jingle was like some of the notes of a robin singing in summer. But they were very short spurts in all these directions—though there was all this variety. Unless you saw the shrike—it would be hard to tell what bird it was. This variety of notes covered considerable time but were sparingly uttered with intervals. It was a decided chinking sound—the clearest strain—suggesting much ice in the stream.

I heard this bird sing once before—but that was also in early spring—or about this time. It is said that they imitate the notes of other birds in order to attract them within its reach. Why then have I never heard them sing in the winter? (I have seen seven or eight of them the past winter quite near.) The birds which it imitated—if it imitated any this morning—were the catbird and the robin—neither of which probably would it catch—and the first is not here to be caught.

Northern shrike in bittersweet

March 8, 1855

I crossed through the swamp south of Boulder Field toward the old dam. Stopping in a sunny and sheltered place on a hillock in the woods for it was raw in the wind, I heard the hasty, shuffling, as if frightened, note of a *robin* from a dense birch wood—a sort of *tche* and then probably it dashed through the birches—and so they fetch the year about. Just from the south shore, perchance, it alighted not in the village street—but in this remote birch wood. This sound reminds me of rainy misty April days in past years. Once or twice before this P.M. I thought I heard one and listened, but in vain.

American robins and sumac

March 9, 1852

The railroad men have now their hands full. I hear and see bluebirds come with the warm wind. The sand is flowing in the Deep Cut.

March 10, 1852

I was reminded, thus morning before I rose of those undescribed ambrosial mornings of summer which I can remember—when a thousand birds were heard gently twittering and ushering in the light—like the argument to a new canto of an epic and heroic poem. The serenity, the infinite promise of such a morning! The song or twitter of birds drips from the leaves like dew. Then there was something divine and immortal in our life.

When I have waked up on my couch in the woods and saw the day dawning, and heard the twittering of the birds. . . .

I see flocks of a dozen bluebirds together. The warble of this bird is innocent and celestial like its color. Saw a sparrow—perhaps a song sparrow—flitting amid the young oaks where the ground was covered with snow. I think that this is an indication that the ground is quite bare a little further south. Probably the spring birds never fly far over a snow-clad country.

March 11, 1856

The sight of a marsh hawk [northern harrier] in Concord meadows is worth more to me than the entry of the allies into Paris. In this sense—I am not ambitious. I do not wish my native soil to become exhausted and run out through neglect.

March 12, 1853

Last night it snowed a sleety snow again and now the ground is whitened with it—and where are gone the bluebirds whose warble was wafted to me so lately like a blue wavelet through the air? . . .

Saw a lark [eastern meadowlark] rise from the railroad causeway and sail on quivering wing over the meadow to alight on a heap of dirt.

Eastern meadowlark

Common grackle

March 13, 1859

7 A M *F hyemalis* [dark-eyed junco] in yard.

Going down railroad—listening *intentionally* I hear far—through the notes of song sparrows (which are very numerous) the song of one or two larks. Also hearing a coarse *chuck* I look up and see four blackbirds whose size and long tails betray them crow blackbirds [common grackles]. Also I hear I am pretty sure the cackle of a pigeon woodpecker [northern flicker]. . . .

I see a small flock of blackbirds flying over—some rising others falling yet all advancing together—one flock but many birds—some silent others *tchucking*—incessant alternation. This harmonious movement as in a dance—this agreeing to differ—makes the charm of the spectacle to me. One bird looks fractional—naked—like a single thread or unraveling from the web to which it belongs. Alternation! Alternation! Heaven and hell!

Here again—in the flight of a bird—its ricochet motion—is that undulation observed in so many materials—as in the mackerel sky.

March 14, 1854

A large company of fox-colored sparrows [fox sparrows] in Heywood's maple swamp close by. I heard their loud sweet canary-like whistle 30 or 40 rods off—sounding richer than anything yet—some on the bushes singing *twee twee-twa twa ter tweer tweer twa*. This is the scheme of it only—there being no dental grit to it. They were shy flitting before me—and I heard a slight susurrus where many were busily scratching amid the leaves of the swamp—without seeing them and also saw many indistinctly. Wilson never heard but one sing—their common note there being a *cheep*.

Fox sparrow

March 15, 1860

Red-tailed hawk

A hen hawk sails away from the wood southward. I get a very fair sight of it sailing overhead. What a perfectly regular and neat outline it presents! an easily recognized figure anywhere. Yet I never see it represented in any books. The exact correspondence of the marks on one side to those on the other—as the black or dark tip of one wing to the other—and the dark line midway the wing. I have no idea that one can get as correct an idea of the form and color of the undersides of a hen hawk's wings by spreading those of a dead specimen in his study—as by looking up at a free and living hawk soaring above him in the fields. The penalty for obtaining a petty knowledge thus dishonestly is that it is less interesting to me generally as it is less significant. Some seeing and admiring the neat figure of the hawk sailing two or three hundred feet above their heads—wish to get nearer and hold it in their hands perchance—not realizing that they can see it best at this distance—better now perhaps than ever they will again.

March 16, 1860

Here is a flock of red-wings—I heard one yesterday—and I see a *female* among these. These are easily distinguished from grackles by the richness and clarity of their notes—as if they were a more developed bird. How handsome as they go by in a checker each with a bright scarlet shoulder! They are not so very shy—but mute when we come near.

I think here are four or five grackles with them which remain when the rest fly. They cover the apple trees like a black fruit.

March 17, 1860

I see a large flock of sheldrakes [common mergansers]—which have probably risen from the pond—go over my head in the woods. A dozen large and compact birds flying with great force and rapidity—spying out the land—eyeing every traveler—fast and far they "steam it" on clipping wings over field and forest—meadow and flood—now here and you hear the whistling

Red-winged blackbird

of their wings—and in a moment they are lost in the horizon. Like swift propellers of the air. Whichever way they are headed that way their wings propel them. What health and vigor they suggest! The life of man seems slow and puny in comparison—reptilian. . . .

How handsome a flock of red-wings—ever changing its oval form as it advances by the rear birds passing the others.

Was not that a marsh hawk, a slate-colored one which I saw flying over Walden Wood with long slender *curving* wings—with a diving zigzag flight? No doubt it was, for I see another, a brown one, the 19th.

March 18, 1858

7 A.M. by river. Almost every bush has its song sparrow this morning and their tinkling strains are heard on all sides. You see them just hopping under the bush or into some other covert as you go by, turning with a jerk this way and that—or they flit away just above the ground which they resemble. It is the prettiest strain I have heard yet.

March 19, 1858

By the river see *distinctly* red-wings—and hear their *conqueree*. They are not associated with grackles. They are an age before their cousins—have attained to clearness and liquidity. They are officers epauletted—the others are rank and file. I distinguish one even by its flight—hovering slowly from treetop to treetop—as if ready to utter its liquid notes. Their whistle is very clear and sharp, while the grackle's is ragged and split.

March 20, 1852

As to the winter birds—those which came here in the winter—I saw first that rusty sparrowlike bird flying in flocks with the smaller sparrows early in the winter and sliding down the grass stems to their seeds, which clucked like a hen. . . Then I saw, about Thanksgiving time and later in the winter the pine grosbeaks—large and carmine, a noble bird—then in midwinter the snow bunting, the white snowbird sweeping low like snowflakes from field to field over the walls and fences. And now within a day or two I have noticed the chubby slate-colored snowbird (*Fringilla hyemalis*?) and I drive the flocks before me on the railroad causeway as I walk. It has two white feathers in its tail.

Dark-eyed junco with red maple buds

It is cold as winter today—the ground still covered with snow—and the stars twinkle as in winter nights.

The fox-colored sparrow is about now.

March 21, 1840

The wild goose [Canada goose] is more a cosmopolite than we. He breaks his fast in Canada—takes a luncheon in the Susquehanna—and plumes himself for the night in a Louisiana bayou.

March 22, 1853

Ruffed grouse

One robin really sings on the elms—even the cockerels crow with new lustiness. Already I hear from the railroad the plaintive strain of a lark or two. They sit now conspicuous on the bare russet ground. The tinkling bubbles of the song sparrow are wafted from distant fence posts. Little rills of song that begin to flow and tinkle as soon as the frost is out of the ground. The blackbird tries to sing as it were with a bone in his throat or to whistle and sing at once. Whither so fast the restless creature—*chuck-chuck* at every rod—and now and then *whistle-ter-ee*. The *chill-lill* of the blue snowbirds is heard again. A partridge [ruffed grouse] goes off on Fair Haven hillside with a sudden whir like the wad of a six-pounder—keeping just level with the tops of the sprouts. These birds and quails [bobwhites] go off like a report.

March 23, 1859

As we sail upward toward the pond, we scare up two or three golden-eyes or whistlers—showing their large black heads and black backs and afterward I watch one swimming not far before us. I see the white spot, amid the black, on the side of his head. . . .

As we entered Well Meadow—we saw a hen hawk perch on the topmost plume of one of the tall pines at the head of the meadow. Soon another appeared—probably its mate—but we looked in vain for a nest there. It was a fine sight their soaring above our heads—presenting a

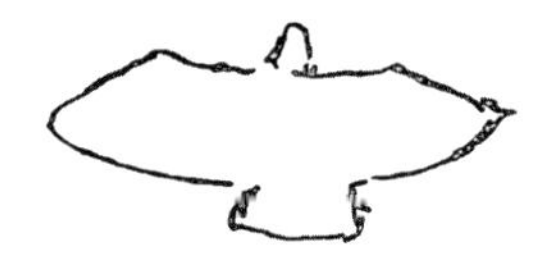

perfect outline and as they came round showing their rust-colored tails with a whitish rump—or as they sailed away from us—that slight teetering or quivering motion of their dark-tipped wings seen edgewise—now on this side now that by which they balanced and directed themselves. These are the most eagle-like of our common hawks. They very commonly perch upon the very topmost plume of a pine—and if motionless are rather hard to distinguish there....

As we sit there we see coming swift and straight northeast along the river valley not seeing us—and therefore not changing his course—a male goosander [common merganser], so near that the green reflections of his head and neck are plainly visible. He looks like a paddle wheel steamer—so oddly painted up black and white and green and moves along swift and straight like one.

March 24, 1858

Returning about 5 P.M. across the Depot Field—I scare up from the ground a flock of about 20 birds which fly low making a short circuit to another part of the field. At first they remind me of baywings [vesper sparrows]—except that they are in a flock—show no white in tail—are I see a little larger—and utter a faint *sveet sveet* merely—a sort of sibilant chip. Starting them again I see that they have black tails—very conspicuous when they pass near. They fly in the flock somewhat like snow buntings—occasionally one surging upward a few feet in pursuit of another—and they alight about where they first were. It is almost impossible to discover them on the ground they squat so flat—and so much resemble it—running amid the stubble. But at length I stand within two rods of one and get a good view of its markings with my glass. They are the *Alauda alpestris* [*Eremophila alpestris*] or shore lark [horned lark], quite a sizable and handsome bird.

Horned larks

March 25, 1858

Fox sparrow

Going across A. Clark's field behind Garfield's—I see many fox-colored sparrows flitting past in a straggling manner into the birch and pitch pine woods on the left—and hear a sweet warble there from time to time. They are busily scratching like hens amid the dry leaves of that wood (not sure why) from time to time the rearmost moving forward one or two at a time—while a few are perched here and there on the lower branches of a birch or other tree—and I hear a very clear and sweet whistling strain—commonly half-finished—from one every two or three minutes. It is too irregular to be readily caught—but methinks begins like *ar tche tche tchear, te tche tchear* etc. etc. but is more clear than these words would indicate. The whole flock is moving along pretty steadily.

There are so many sportsmen out that the ducks have no rest on the Great Meadows which are not half covered with water. They sit uneasy on the water looking about—without feeding—and I see one man endeavor to approach a flock—crouchingly through the meadow for half a mile—with india rubber boots on—where the water is often a foot deep. This has been going on on these meadows ever since the town was settled—and will go on as long as ducks settle here.

You might frequently say of a poet away from home that he was as mute as a bird of passage—uttering a mere *chip* from time to time—but follow him to his true habitat—and you shall not know him he will sing so melodiously.

March 26, 1853

Saw about 10 A.M. a gaggle of geese 43 in number—in a very perfect harrow flying northeasterly. One side the harrow was a little longer than the other. They appeared to be four or five feet apart. At first I heard faintly as I stood by Minott's gate—borne to me from the southwest through the confused sounds of the village—the indistinct honking of geese. I was somewhat surprised to find that Mr. Loring at his house should have heard and seen the same flock. I should think that the same flock was commonly seen and heard from the distance of a mile east and west. It is remarkable that we *commonly* see geese go over in the spring about 10 o'clock in the morning—as if they were accustomed to stop for the night at some place southward whence they reached us at that time. Goodwin saw six geese in Walden about the same time.

March 27, 1858

We hear a squeaking note—as if made by a pump—and presently see four or five great herring gulls wheeling about. Sometimes they make a sound like the scream of a hen hawk. They are shaped somewhat like a very thick white rolling pin sharpened at both ends. At length they alight near the ducks.

March 28, 1856

Sam Barrett tells me that a boy caught a crow in his neighborhood the other day in a trap set for mink. Its leg was broken. He brought it home under his arm and laid it down in a shop thinking to keep it there alive. It looked up sidewise as it lay seemingly helpless on the floor—but, the door being open—all at once to their surprise it lifted itself on its wings and flitted out and away without the least trouble. Many crows have been caught in mink traps the past winter, they have been compelled to visit the few openings in brooks etc. so much for food.

American crow

March 29, 1853

On approaching the island [near Cheney's boathouse], I am surprised to hear the scolding cackle-like note of the pigeon woodpecker—a prolonged loud sound somewhat like one note of the robin. This was the tapper—on the old hollow aspen which the small woodpeckers so much frequent. Unless the latter make *exactly* the same sound with the former—then the pigeon woodpecker has come!! But I could not get near enough to distinguish his size and colors. He went up the Assabet and I heard him cackling and tapping far ahead....

Northern flicker

It would be worth the while to attend more to the different notes of the blackbirds. Methinks I may have seen the female red-wing within a *day or two*—or what are these purely black ones without the red shoulder? It is pleasant to see them scattered about on the drying meadow. The red-wings will stand close to the water's edge looking larger than usual—with their red shoulders very distinct and handsome in that position—and sing *okolee*—or *bob-y-lee*—or whatnot. Others on the tops of trees over your head—out of a fuzzy beginning spit forth a clear shrill whistle incessantly—for what purpose I don't know. Others on the elms over the water utter still another note, each time lifting their wings slightly. Others are flying across the stream with a loud *char-r, char-r*. . . .

Would it not be well to carry a spyglass in order to watch these shy birds—such as ducks and hawks? In some respects methinks it would be better than a gun. The latter brings them nearer dead, but the former, alive. You can identify the species better by killing the bird—because it was a dead specimen that was so minutely described—but you can study the habits and appearance best in the living specimen.

March 30, 1858

Landing at Bittern Cliff—I went round through the woods to get sight of ducks on the pond.

Creeping down through the woods I reached the rocks and saw 15 or 20 sheldrakes scattered about. The full-plumaged males—conspicuously black and white—and often swimming in pairs—appeared to be the most wary—keeping furthest out. Others with much less white and duller black were very busily fishing just north the inlet of the pond—where there is about three feet of water—and others still playing and preening themselves. These ducks whose tame representatives are so sluggish and deliberate in their motions—were full of activity. A party of these ducks fishing and playing is a very lively scene. On one side for instance you will see a party of eight or ten busily diving and most of the time under water—not rising high when they come up—and soon plunging again. The whole surface will be in commotion there though no ducks may be seen. I saw one come up with a large fish—whereupon all the rest as they successively came to the surface gave chase to it—while it held its prey over the water in its bill—and they pursued with a great rush and clatter a dozen or more rods over the surface making a great furrow in the water—but there being some trees in the way I could not see the issue.

March 31, 1858

I am not sure—but I heard a pine warbler day before yesterday—and from what a boy asks me about a yellowbird [yellow warbler] chick he saw there I think it likely. Just after sundown I see a large flock of geese in a perfect harrow cleaving their way toward the northeast. With Napoleonic tactics splitting the forces of winter.

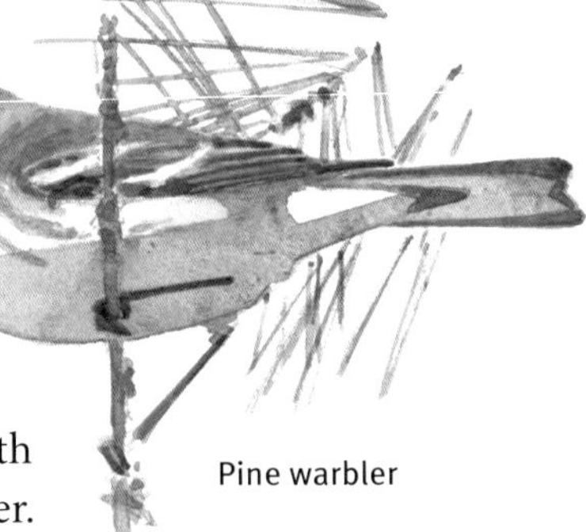

Pine warbler

APRIL

April 1, 1852

I hear a robin singing on the woods south of Hosmer's just before sunset. It is a sound associated with New England village life. It brings to my thoughts summer evenings when the children are playing in the yards before the doors and their parents conversing at the open windows. It foretells all this now before those summer hours are come.

As I come over the Turnpike, the song sparrow's jingle comes up from every part of the meadow as native as the tinkling rills—or the blossoms of the spirea. The meadow-sweet—soon to spring. Its *cheep* is like the sound of opening buds. The sparrow is continually singing on the alders along the brookside while the sun is continually setting.

April 2, 1852

6 A.M. To the riverside and Merrick's pasture. The sun is up. The water on the meadows is perfectly smooth and placid, reflecting the hills and clouds and trees. The air is full of the notes of birds—song sparrows, red-wings, robins (singing a strain), bluebirds—and I hear also a lark. As if all the earth had burst forth into song. The influence of this April morning has reached them for they live out-of-doors all the night, and there is no danger that they will oversleep themselves such a morning. A few weeks ago, before the birds had come there came to my mind in the night the twittering sound of birds in the early dawn of a spring morning—a semi-prophecy of it—and last night I attended mentally as if I heard the spraylike dreaming sound of the midsummer frog—and realized how glorious and full of revelations it was. Expectation may amount to prophecy.

Eastern meadowlark

April 3, 1858

Going downtown this morning—I am surprised by the rich strain of the purple finch—from the elms. Three or four have arrived and lodged against the elms of our street—which runs east and west across their course—and they are now mingling their loud and rich strain with that of the tree sparrows—robins—bluebirds etc.

The hearing of this note implies some improvement in the acoustics of the air. It reminds me of that genial state of the air when the elms are in bloom. They sit still over the street and make a business of warbling. They advertise me surely of some additional warmth and serenity. How their note rings over the roofs of the village! You wonder that even the sleepers are not awakened by it—to inquire who is there—and yet probably not another than myself in all the town observes their coming and not half a dozen ever distinguished them in their lives. And yet the very mob of the town know the hard names of Germanians or Swiss families which once sang here or elsewhere.

Purple finch

April 4, 1855

The rows of white spots near the end of the wings of the downy [woodpecker] remind me of the lacings on the skirts of a soldier's coat.

April 5, 1853

The bluebird comes to us bright in his vernal dress as a bridegroom. (Cleared up at noon, making a day and a half of rain.) Has he not got new feathers then. Brooks says "the greater number of birds renew their plumage in autumn only." If they have two moults—spring and autumn—there is still but one of the wings and tail feathers. . . .

I have noticed the few phoebes—not to mention other birds—mostly near the river. Is it not because of the greater abundance of insects there—those early moths or ephemerae? As these and other birds are most numerous there, the red-tailed hawk is there to catch them?

Eastern phoebe

April 6, 1855

Yesterday I was wishing that I could find a dead duck floating on the water, as I had found muskrats and a hare—and now I see something bright and reflecting the light from the edge of the alders five or six rods off. Can it be a duck? I can hardly believe my eyes. I am near enough to see its green head and neck. I am delighted to find a perfect specimen of the *Mergus merganser* or goosander—undoubtedly shot yesterday by the Fast Day sportsmen—and I take a small flattened shot from its wing—flattened against the wing bone apparently. The wing is broken and it is shot through the head. It is a perfectly fresh and very beautiful bird—and as I raise it, I get sight of its long slender vermilion bill (color of red sealing wax) and its clean bright orange legs and feet—and then of its perfectly smooth and spotlessly pure white breast and belly tinged with a faint salmon (or say tinged with a delicate buff inclining to salmon). This according to Wilson is one of the mergansers or fisher ducks of which there are nine or ten species and we have four—in America.

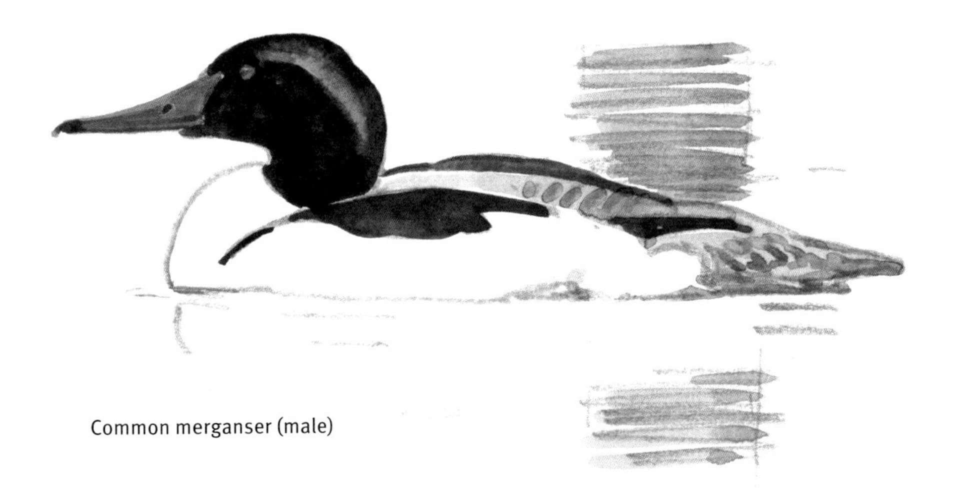

Common merganser (male)

April 7, 1855

I skinned my duck [merganser] yesterday and stuffed it today. It is wonderful that a man having undertaken such an enterprise ever persevered in it to the end—and equally wonderful that he succeeded. To skin a bird—drawing backward wrong side out over the legs and wings down to the base of the mandibles! Who would expect to see a smooth feather again? This skin was very tender on the breast. I should have done better had I stuffed it at once or turned it back before the skin became stiff. Look out not to cut the ear and eyelid. But what a pot-bellied thing is a stuffed bird compared even with the fresh dead one I found! It looks no longer like an otter—like a swift diver but a mere waddling duck. How perfectly the vent of a bird is covered! There is no mark externally.

Bald eagle

April 8, 1854

Saw a large bird sail along over the edge of Wheeler's cranberry meadow just below Fair Haven—which I at first thought a gull, but with my glass found it was a hawk and had a perfectly white head and tail and broad black or blackish wings. It sailed and circled along over the low cliff and the crows dived at it in the field of my glass—and I saw it well both above and beneath as it turned—and then it passed off to hover over the Cliffs at a greater height. It was undoubtedly a white-headed eagle [bald eagle]. It was to the eye but a large hawk.

April 9, 1856

The red-wing's *o'gurgle-ee-e* is in singular harmony with the sound and impression of the lapsing stream or the smooth swelling flood beneath his perch. He gives expression to the flood. The water reaches far in amid the trees on which he sits—and they seem like a water organ played on by the flood—the sound rises up through the pipes.

Red-winged blackbird

April 10, 1854

There are many [Wilson's] snipes now feeding in the meadows—which you come close upon and then they go off with hoarse *cr-rr-ack cr-r-r-ack*. They dive down suddenly from a considerable height sometimes when they alight.

Rusty blackbird

April 11, 1856

Going up the railroad I see a male and female rusty grackle [rusty blackbird] alight on an oak near me—the latter apparently a flaxen brown—with a black tail. She looks like a different species of bird. Wilson had heard only a *tchuck* from the grackle—but this male who was courting his mate—broke into incipient warbles—like a bubble burst as soon as it came to the surface—it was so aerated. Its air would not be fixed long enough.

April 12, 1858

Returning on the railroad the noon train down passed us opposite the old maid Hosmer's house. In the woods just this side we came upon a partridge standing on the track between the rails over which the cars had just passed. She had evidently been run down—but though a few small feathers were scattered along for a dozen rods beyond her—and she looked a little ruffled—she was apparently more disturbed in mind than body. I took her up and carried her one side to a safer place. At first she made no resistance—but at length fluttered out of my hands—and ran *two or three feet*. I had to take her up again and carry and drive her further off—and left her standing with head erect as at first—as if beside herself. She was not lame—and I suspect no wing was broken. I did not suspect that this swift wild bird was ever run down by the cars. We have an account in the newspapers of every cow and calf that is run over—but not of the various wild creatures who meet with that accident. It may be many generations before the partridges learn to give the cars a sufficiently wide berth.

April 13, 1860

At first I had felt disinclined to make this excursion up the Assabet—but it distinctly occurred to me that, perhaps if I come against my will as it were—to look at the sweetgale as a matter [of] business—I might discover something else interesting—as when I discovered the sheldrake. As I was paddling past the uppermost hemlocks I saw two peculiar and plump birds near me on the bank there—which reminded me of the cow blackbird [brown-headed cowbird] and of the oriole at first. I saw at once that they were new to me—and guessed that they were crossbills—which was the case—*male* and *female*. The former was dusky greenish (through a glass) orange and red, the orange etc. on head breast and rump. The vent white—dark large bill. The female more of a dusky slate color and yellow instead of orange and red. They were very busily eating the seeds of the hemlock—whose cones were strewn over the ground and they were very fearless—allowing me to approach quite near.

When I returned this way I looked for them again—and at the larger hemlocks heard a peculiar note *cheep, cheep, cheep, cheep*, in the rhythm of a fish hawk [osprey] but faster and rather loud—and looking up saw them fly to the north side and alight on the top of a swamp white oak—while I sat in my boat close under the south bank. But immediately they recrossed and went to feeding on the bank within a rod of me. They were very parrot-like both in color (especially the male)—greenish and orange etc. and in their manner of feeding—holding the hemlock cones in one claw and rapidly extracting the seeds with their bills. Thus trying one cone after another very fast. But they kept their bills agoing that near as they were I did not distinguish the *cross*. I should have looked at them in *profile*. At last the two hopped within six feet of me and one

Red crossbill

within four feet—and they were coming still nearer—as if partly from curiosity—though nibbling the cones all the while when my chain fell down and rattled loudly for the wind shook the boat—and they flew off a rod.

April 14, 1852

The different parts of Fair Haven Pond—the pond, the meadow beyond the buttonbush and willow curve, the island, and the meadow between the island and mainland with its own defining lines—are all parted off like the parts of a mirror. A fish hawk is calmly sailing over all looking for his prey. The gulls are all gone now, though the water is high, but I can see the motions of a muskrat on the calm sunny surface a great way off. So perfectly calm and beautiful and yet no man looking at it this morning but myself. It is pleasant to see the zephyrs strike the smooth surface of the pond from time to time. And a darker shade ripple over it.

The streams break up, the ice goes to the sea. Then sails the fish hawk overhead looking for his prey.

Herring gull at sunset

April 15, 1852

I do *not remember* to have seen them [gulls] over or in our river meadows when there was not ice there.

They come annually a-fishing here like royal hunters. To remind us of the sea—and that our town after all lies but further up a creek of the universal sea—above the head of the tide. So ready is a deluge to overwhelm our lands as the gulls to circle hither in the spring freshets. To see a gull beating high over our meadowy flood in chill and windy March is akin to seeing a mackerel schooner on the coast. It is the nearest approach to sailing vessels in our scenery. I never saw one at Walden.

O how it salts our fresh, our sweet-watered Fair Haven all at once to see this sharp-beaked greedy sea bird beating over it! For a while the water is brackish to my eyes. It is merely some herring pond—and if I climb the eastern bank I expect to see the Atlantic there covered with countless sails. Whoever thought that Walden's blue and emerald water was ever prophaned by wing of gull or cormorant. We are so far maritime—do not dwell beyond the range of the seagoing gull, the littoral birds. Does not the gull come up after those suckers which I see? He is never to me perfectly in harmony with the scenery—but like the high water something unusual.

April 16, 1855

5 A.M. to Hill. Clear and cool—a frost whitens the ground—yet a mist hangs over the village. There is a thin ice reaching a foot from the water's edge—which the earliest rays will melt. I scare up several snipes feeding on the meadow's edge. It is remarkable how they conceal themselves when they alight on a bare spit of the meadow. I look with my glass to where one alighted four rods off—and at length detect its head rising amid the cranberry vines and withered grass blades which last it closely resembled in color—with its eye steadily fixed on me.

April 17, 1852

Gilpin says—"As the wheeling motion of the gull is beautiful, so also is the figured flight of the goose, the duck, and the widgeon; all of which are highly ornamental to coast-views, bays, and estuaries." A flight of ducks adds to the wildness of our wildest river scenery. . . .

These deep withdrawn bays—like that toward Well Meadow—are resorts for many a shy flock of ducks. They are very numerous this afternoon. We scare them up every quarter of a mile—mostly the whitish duck, which Brown thinks the golden-eye (we call them whistlers) and also black ducks, perchance also sheldrakes. They are quite shy—swim rapidly away far into the pond. A flock which we surprised in the smooth bay of Well Meadow divided and showed much cunning—dodging under the shore to avoid us. . . .

The first flowers are not the highest-scented—as catkins—as the first birds are not the finest singers—as the blackbirds and song sparrows etc. The beginnings of the year are humble.

Common goldeneyes

Palm warbler

April 18, 1854

The male yellow redpoll's [palm warbler] breast and underparts are of a peculiarly splendid and lively yellow—glowing. It is remarkable that they too are found about willows etc. along the water.

April 19, 1852

What comes flapping low with heavy wing over the middle of the flood. Is it an eagle or a fish hawk? Ah, now he is betrayed, I know not by what motion—a great gull [herring gull]. Right in the eye of the storm. He holds not a steady course—but suddenly he dashes upward even like the surf of the sea which he frequents—showing the undersides of his long, pointed wings, on which do I not see two white spots? He suddenly beats upward thus as if to surmount the airy billows by a slanting course as the teamster surmounts a slope. The swallow too flies fantastically and luxuriously and leisurely—doubling some unseen corners in the sky. Here is a gull then long after ice in the river. It is a fine sight to see this noble bird leisurely advancing right in the face of the storm.

April 20, 1854

The sound of the snipes winnowing the evening air now at starlight invisible but for an instant high over the meadows is heard far into the village *hoo hoo hoo hoo hoo hoo* rising higher and higher or dying away as they circle round. A ghostly sound.

Wilson's snipe

April 21, 1854

The song of the purple finch on the elms (he also frequents firs and spruce) is rich and continuous—like but fainter and more rapid than that of a robin. Some of the *cherruwit* in it and a little of the warble of the martin.

April 22, 1857

But few birds are seen—only a crow or two teetering along the water's edge looking for its food—with its large clumsy head—and on unusually long legs—as if stretched—or its pants pulled up to keep it from the wet—and now flapping off with some large morsel in its bill...

Hermit thrush

April 23, 1856

Along the shore by Dove Rock I hear a faint *tseep* like a fox-colored sparrow—and looking sharp detect upon a maple a white-throated sparrow. It soon flies to the ground amid the birches two or three rods distant—a plump-looking bird and with its bright white and yellow marks on the head distinctly—separated from the slate-color—methinks the most brilliant of the sparrows.

April 24, 1856

Returning in the low wood just this side the first Second Division Brook—near the meadow—see a brown bird flit—and behold my hermit thrush—with one companion flitting silently through the birches. I saw the fox-color on his tail coverts—as well as the brown streaks on the breast. Both kept up a constant jerking of the tail as they sat on their perches....

Goodwin shot about 6 P.M. and brought to me a cinereous coot *Fulica Americana* which was flying over the willows at Willow Bay—where the water now runs up.

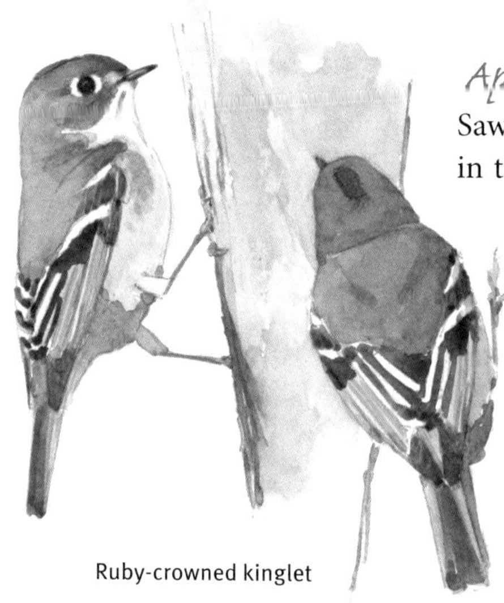
Ruby-crowned kinglet

April 25, 1854

Saw a ruby-crested wren [ruby-crowned kinglet] in the woods near Goose Pond. . . . It sounded far off—and like an imitation of a robin—a long strain and often repeated. I was quite near it before I was aware of it sounding still like a faint imitation of a robin—and of a golden robin [Baltimore oriole] which later I often mistook for him.

Some chickadees and yellow redpolls were first apparent, then my wren on the pitch pines and young oaks. He appeared curious to observe me. A very interesting and active little fellow darting about amid the treetops—and his song quite remarkable and rich and loud for his size. Begins with a very fine note before its pipes are filled—not audible at a little distance—then *woriter weter* etc. etc. winding up with *teter teter* all clear and round. His song is comical and reminds me of the thrasher. This was at 4 P.M. when most birds do not sing. I saw it yesterday pluming itself and stretching its little wings. Our smallest bird methinks except the hummingbird.

April 26, 1854

The swamp sparrow—very dark with chestnut and black, and quirk of the tail—flits shyly under the alders along the causeway. Hides or lurks behind the trunks like song sparrow and hardly rests a moment in one place.

Swamp sparrow

April 27, 1856

The tapping of a woodpecker is made a more remarkable and emphatic sound—by the hollowness of the trunk—the expanse of water which conducts the sound—and the morning hour at which I commonly hear it.

I think that the pigeon woodpeckers must be building they frequent the old aspen now so much.

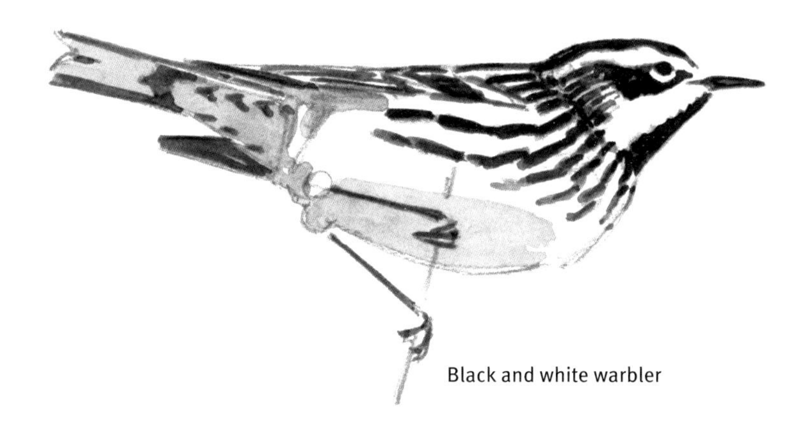

Black and white warbler

April 28, 1856

I hear today frequently the *seezer seezer seezer* of the black and white creeper [black and white warbler]—or what I have referred to that from J. P. Brown's wood bounding on Dugan. It is not a note nor a bird to attract attention—only suggesting still warmer weather—that the season has revolved so much further. See, but not yet hear, the familiar chewink [eastern towhee] amid the dry leaves—amid the underwood on the meadow's edge.

April 29, 1855

This morning it snows—but the ground is not yet whitened. This will probably take the cold out of the air. Many chip-birds [chipping sparrows] are feeding in the yard—and one baywing. The latter incessantly scratches like a hen all the while looking about for foes. The bay on its wings is not obvious except when it opens them. The white circle about the eye is visible afar. Now it makes a business of pluming itself—doubling prettily upon itself—now touching the root of its tail—now thrusting its

Vesper sparrow

head under its wing—now between its wing and back above—and now between its legs and its belly—and now it drops flat on its breast and belly and spreads and shakes its wings, now stands up and repeatedly shakes its wings. It is either cleaning itself of dirt acquired in scratching and feeding—for its feet are black with mud—or it is oiling its feathers thus. It is rather better concealed by its color than the chip-bird with its chestnut crown—and light breast. The chip-bird scratches but slightly and rarely—it finds what it wants on the surface—keeps its head down more steadily—not looking about. I see the baywing eat some worms. . . .

Paddling slowly along, I see five or six snipes within four or five rods feeding on the meadow just laid bare—or in the shallow and grassy water. This dark damp cold day they do not mind me. View them with my glass. How the ends of their wings curve upward. They do not thrust their bills clear down commonly—but wade and nibble at something amid the grass, apparently on the surface of the water. Sometimes it seems to be the grass itself—sometimes on the surface of the bare meadow. They are not now thrusting their bills deep in the mud. They have dark ash or slate-colored breasts. At length they take a little alarm and rise with a sort of rippling whistle or peep—a *little like* a robin's peep—but faint and soft—and then alight within a dozen rods. I hear often at night a very different harsh squeak from them and another squeak much like the nighthawk's—and also the booming.

April 30, 1855

I observed yesterday that the barn swallows confined themselves to one place about 15 rods in diameter in Willow Bay about the sharp rock. They kept circling about and flying up the stream (the wind easterly) about six inches above the water (it was cloudy and almost raining)—yet I could not perceive any insects there. Those myriads of little fuzzy gnats mentioned on the 21st and 28th must afford an abundance of food to insectivorous birds. Many new birds should have arrived about the 21st. There were plenty of myrtle birds [yellow-rumped warblers] and yellow redpolls where the gnats were. The swallows were confined to this space when I passed up and were still there when I returned, an hour and a half later. I saw them nowhere else. They uttered only a slight twitter from time to time and when they turned out for each other on meeting. Getting their meal seemed to be made a social affair. Pray how long will they continue to circle thus without resting?

Barn swallow on nest

MAY

May 1, 1852

I hear the first towhee finch. He says *to-wee—to-wee*. And another—much farther off than I supposed when I went in search of him—says *whip your ch-r-r-r r-r-r* with a metallic ring. I hear the first catbird also—mewing—and the wood thrush which still thrills me—a sound to be heard in a new country from one side of a clearing. I think I heard an ovenbird just now—*wicher—wicher—whicher—wich*. I am on the Cliff. It is about six. The flicker cackles. I hear a woodpecker tapping. The tinkle of the huckleberry bird [field sparrow] comes up from the shrub oak plain. He commonly lives away from the habitations of men.

Eastern towhee

In retired bushy fields—and sproutlands. A partridge bursts away from under the rock below me on quivering wings like some moths I have seen. We have then flowers and the song of birds before the woods leave out—like poetry.

Yellow-rumped warbler

May 2, 1852

I am pretty sure that is the myrtle bird I see and hear on the Corner road—picking the blossoms of the maple—with the yellow crown and black throat or cheeks. It sings *pe-te-te-te-ter twé* emphasizing the last and repeating the second, third, and fourth fast.

May 3, 1852

Hear the first brown thrasher, two of them. Minott says he heard one yesterday—but does he know it from a catbird? They drown all the rest. He says *cherruwit cherruwit—go ahead—go ahead go ahead give it to him give it to him* etc. etc. etc.

Brown thrasher

Black-throated blue warbler

May 4, 1853

The woods and fields next them now ring with the silver jingle of the field sparrow—the medley of the brown thrasher—the honest *qui vive* of the chewink—or his jingle from the top of a low copse tree while his mate scratches in the dry leaves beneath. The black and white creeper is hopping along the oak boughs head downward—pausing from time to time to utter its note like a fine delicate saw—sharpening—and ever and anon rises clear over all the smooth rich melody of the wood thrush. Could that have been a jay? I think it was some large, uncommon woodpecker that uttered that very loud strange cackling note. . . .

The indigo bird and mate dark throat and light beneath and white spot on wings which is not described. [From the description, these were not indigo buntings but a male and female black-throated blue warbler.] A hoarse note and rapid the first two or three syllables—*twe twe twee* dwelling on the last or *twe-twe, twe, twee e* or as if an *r* in it *tre* etc. not musical.

Field sparrow

May 5, 1852

Hear on the elms in the street for the first time that I remember—the purple finch (without the crimson) singing loud like a warbling vireo—but with more variety. Hear also this morning in the village the chickadee's fine ringing air-possessing *tull a lull tull a lull*. Is this the third note of this bird—and confined to this season. Heard it the morning of the brown thrasher. The other afternoon I could not hear the birds sing, the wind in the woods made such a noise.

May 6, 1857

A beautiful and warm day. I go to build an arbor for R. W. E. [Ralph Waldo Emerson]. The thrasher has been heard this A.M. While at work I hear the bobolink and methinks peetweet [spotted sandpiper] along the brook (surely see it on the 9th).

May 7, 1855

. . . I observed a mid-sized red oak standing a little aslant on the sidehill over the swamp—with a pretty large hole in one side about 15 feet from the ground where apparently a limb on which a felled tree lodged had been cut some years before and so broke out a cavity. I thought that such a hole was too good a one not to be improved by some inhabitant of the wood. Perhaps the gray squirrels I had just seen had their nest there—or was not the entrance big enough to admit a screech owl. So I thought I would tap on it and put my ear to the trunk—and see if I could hear anything stirring within it but I heard nothing. Then I concluded to look into it. So I shinned up—and when I reached up one hand to the hole to pull myself up by it the thought passed through my mind perhaps something may take hold my fingers—but nothing did. The first limb was nearly opposite to the hole—and, resting on this I looked in and to my great surprise there squatted filling the hole which was about six inches deep and five to six wide,— salmon-brown bird not so big as a partridge seemingly asleep within three inches of the top and close to my face. It was a minute or two before I made it out to be an owl. It was a salmon-brown or fawn (?) above—the feathers shafted with small blackish brown somewhat hastate (?) marks—*grayish* toward the ends of the wings and tail as far as I could see. A large white circular space about or behind eye banded in rear by a pretty broad (⅓ of an inch) and quite conspicuous perpendicular *dark*

Eastern screech owl

brown stripe. Egret [tuft of feathers] say 1¼ inches long, sharp triangular reddish brown without mainly. It lay crowded in that small space—with its tail somewhat bent up—and one side of its head turned up with one egret—and its large dark eye open only by a long slit about 1⁄16 of an inch wide—visible breathing. After a little while I put in one hand and stroked it repeatedly whereupon it reclined its head a little lower and closed its eye entirely. Though curious to know what was under it I disturbed it no farther at that time.

May 8, 1860

The *simple peep peep* of the peetweet as it flies away from the shore before me sounds hollow and rather mournful reminding me of the seashore and its wrecks. And when I smell the fresh odor of our marshes—the resemblance is increased.

Blue-headed vireo on nest

May 9, 1858

See, in the Holden Swamp wood the bird of May 3d. It has sly and inquisitive ways holding down its head and looking at me at some distance off. It has a distinct white line along the bill and about the eyes—and no yellow there, as is said of the white-eyed vireo—and I am now inclined to think it the *solitary vireo* (?) [blue-headed vireo] whose song is not described and which is considered rare. I should say it had a blue-slate head—and, I note, a distinct yellowish *vent*—which none of the vireos are allowed to have!! The sides of the body are distinctly yellow—but there is none at all on the throat or breast.

May 10, 1853

I hear and have for a week in the woods the note of one or more small birds somewhat like a yellowbird's; what is it? Is it the redstart? I now see one of these. The first I have distinguished.... As I sit it inquisitively hops nearer and nearer. It is one of the election birds of rare colors which I can remember—mingled dark and reddish. This reminds me that I supposed much more variety and fertility in Nature—before I had learned the numbers and the names of each order. I find that I had expected such fertility in our Concord woods alone—as not even the completest museum of stuffed birds of all the forms and colors from all parts of the world comes up to.

American redstart

May 11, 1853

I nearly stepped upon a song sparrow and a striped snake at the same time. The bird fluttered away almost as if detained. I thought it was a case of charming without doubt—and should think so still if I had not found her nest with five eggs there which will account for her being so near the snake that was about to devour her.

May 12, 1855

Watched a black and white creeper from Bittern Cliff. A very neat and active bird—exploring the limbs on all sides—and looking three or four ways almost at once for insects. Now and then it raises its head a *little*, opens its bill and without closing it utters its faint *seeser seeser seeser*. From beyond the orchard saw a large bird *far* over the Cliff Hill—which with my glass I soon made out to be a fish hawk advancing. Even at that distance half a mile off I distinguished its gull-like body (pirate-like fishing body fit to dive) and that its wings did not curve upward at the ends like a hen hawk's (at least I couldn't see that they did) but rather hung down. It came on steadily, bent on fishing—with long and *heavy* undulating wings with an *easy sauntering flight*—over the river to the pond—and hovering over Pleasant Meadow a long time—hovering from time to time in one spot—when more than a hundred feet high—then making a very short circle or two and hovering again—then sauntering off against the woodside. At length he reappeared, passed downward over the shrub oak plain and alighted on an oak (of course now bare) standing this time apparently lengthwise on the limb. Soon took to wing again and went to fishing down the stream 100 feet high. When just below Bittern Cliff I observed by its motions that it observed something. It made a broad circle of observation in its course—lowering itself somewhat then by one or two steep sidewise flights it reached the water—and as near as intervening trees would let me see skimmed over it and endeavored to clutch its prey in passing. It failed the first time but probably succeeded the second. Then it leisurely winged its way to a tall bare tree on the east side of the Cliffs and there we left it apparently pluming itself. It had a very white belly—and indeed appeared all white beneath its body. I saw broad black lines between the white crown and throat.

Osprey

May 13, 1856

In the swallow holes behind Dennis' I find two more dead bank swallows—and one on the sand beneath—and the feathers of two more which some creature has eaten. . . . It chanced that each one of two I tried weighed between 5 and 6 sixteenths of an ounce—or between 5 and 6 drams avoirdupois. This seems to be the average weight—or say 6 drams because they have pined a little. A man who weighs 150 pounds weighs 6,400 times as much as one.

The wing of one contains about seven square inches—the body about five—one whole bird 19. If a man were to be provided with wings etc. in proportion to his weight—they would measure about 844 square feet and one wing would cover 311 feet or be about 33 feet long by 14 wide. This is to say nothing of his muscle.

May 14, 1852

First kingbird. Its voice and flight relate it to the swallow. . . .

These willows have yellow bark—bear yellow flowers and yellowish green leaves—and are now haunted by the summer yellowbird and Maryland yellow-throat. They see this now conspicuous mass of yellowish verdure at a distance and fly to it. . . .

Saw a whippoorwill sitting in the path in woods on the mill road—the brown mottled bird. It flutters off fluidly with slow soft flight. Most birds are silent in the storm.

May 15, 1855

Minott says that some years ago, maybe 10 or 15, a man in Bedford climbed to an owl's nest (probably a cat owl's [great horned owl]) and the owl took out one of his eyes and nearly killed him. He read it in the papers.

Great horned owl

May 16, 1858

See again the warbler of yesterday. All bright yellow beneath and apparently bluish slate above—but I do not see it well. Its note, with little variation, is like *twit twit, twit twit, twitter twitter twe.* It must be the particolored warbler [northern parula].

May 17, 1853

Everything has sensibly advanced during the warm and moist night—some trees as the small maples in the street already look verdurous. The air has not sensibly cooled much. The chimney swallows [chimney swifts] are busily skimming low over the river and just touching the water without regard to me—as a week ago they did—and as they circle back overhead to repeat the experiment, I hear a sharp snap or short rustling of their wings.

May 18, 1860

A hairy woodpecker betrays its hole in an apple tree by its anxiety. The ground is strewn with the chips it has made over a large space. The hole, so far as I can see, is exactly like that of the downy woodpecker—the entrance (though not so round) and the conical form within above—only larger.

The bird scolds at me from a dozen rods off.

May 19, 1856

I see running along the water's edge on the Island Neck—amid the twigs a new bird slender and somewhat warbler-like—but plainly a *Turdus*—with a deep dark chocolate brown back (apparently uniformly)—apparently cream-colored beneath handsomely and abundantly spotted with dark brown—vent white—light flesh-colored legs—yellowish or cream colored line over eyes. Methinks it teetered or wagged its tail—flew soon and was quite shy. I think it must have been the *Turdus aquaticus* [waterthrush] from its dark chocolate brown back—and running along the water's edge—feel pretty *sure*—yet that is said to have white (?) over eye. I lost it before I had examined fully. Quite a discovery. *Vide* golden-crowned thrush [ovenbird] carefully.

May 20, 1856

Young blackpoll warbler bathing

I see, on a locust in the locust burying ground the *Sylvia striata* or blackpoll warbler—busily picking about the locust buds and twigs. Black head and above with olive (green) wings and two white bars, white all beneath with a very distinct black line from throat to shoulders—flesh-colored legs—bill dark above light beneath. Hear no note. Saw it well.

May 21, 1852

The catbird sings like a robin sometimes—sometimes like a blackbird's sprayey warble. There is more of squeak or mew and also of clear *whistle* than in the thrasher's note.

May 22, 1854

A hummingbird dashes by like a loud bumblebee.

Gray catbird

Waterthrushes

May 23, 1860

I see on the white maples and afterward running along the shore close to the water—at different times three or four water thrushes—water wagtails, *Turdus Noveboracensis*. By its lurking along the waterside it might be mistaken by some at first for the song sparrow. It is considerably like the golden-crowned thrush—but it has a *distinct buffish-white* line over the eye—and the breast and sides distinctly striped with dark. *All* above uniform olive brown. It may be distinguished at a distance from a sparrow—by its wagging motion *teetering* on its perch. It persistently runs along the shore peetweet- and song-sparrow-like—running like a rail *around* the tussocks and other obstacles and appearing again at the water's edge. It was not very shy. We very easily kept along two rods off it, while it was amid the buttonbushes.

May 24, 1855

Hear a rose-breasted grosbeak—at first thought it a tanager—but soon I perceived its more *clear* and instrumental—should say whistle if one could whistle like a flute—a noble singer reminding me also of a robin—clear loud and flute-like—on the oaks hillside south of Great Fields. Black all above except white on wing—with a triangular red mark on breast but, as I saw, all white beneath this. . . . Song not so sweet as clear and strong. Saw it fly off and catch an insect like a flycatcher. . . .

Heard a purple finch sing more than one minute without pause—loud and rich on an elm over the street—another singing very faintly on a neighboring elm.

Rose-breasted grosbeak

May 25, 1855

Apparently yellowbirds' nests just completed—one by stone bridge causeway—another in birch by mud turtle meadow. *Veronica peregrina* [purslane speedwell] in Mackay's strawberries how long? Most of the robins' nests I have examined this year had three eggs—clear bluish green.

A chip-bird's nest on a balm of Gilead eight feet high—between the main stem and a twig or two with four very pale blue-green eggs with a sort of circle of brown black spots about larger end.

Red-wing's nest with four eggs—white *very faintly tinged* with perhaps green and curiously and neatly marked with brown black spots and lines on the large end. Red-wings now generally beginning to lay. . . .

Scared a screech owl out of an apple tree on hill—flew swiftly off at first like a pigeon woodpecker and lit nearby facing me— was instantly visited and spied at by a brown thrasher. Then flew into a hole high in a hickory nearby—the thrasher following close to the tree. It was reddish or ferruginous.

May 26, 1855

At the screech owl's nest I now find two young slumbering almost uniformly gray above—about five inches long—with little dark grayish tufts for incipient horns (?). Their heads about as broad as their bodies. I handle them without their stirring or opening their eyes. There are the feathers of a small bird and the leg of the *Mus leucopus* [white-footed mouse] in the nest. . . .

In the meanwhile hear another note—very *smart* and somewhat sprayey rasping—*tshrip tshrip tshrip tshrip* or five or six times with equal force each time. The bird hops near directly over my head. It is black with a large *white* mark forward on wings—and a fiery orange throat above and below eye and line on crown—yellowish beneath—white vent—forked tail, dusky legs and bill. Holds its wings (which are light beneath) loosely. It inclines to examine about the lower branches of the white pines or midway up. The Blackburnian warbler very plainly—whose note Nuttall knows nothing about.

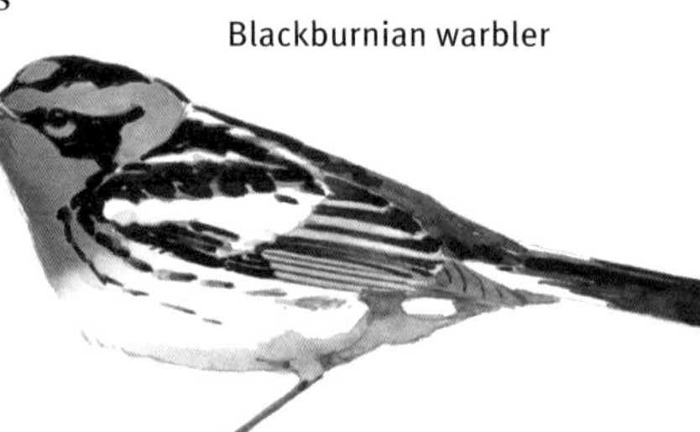

Blackburnian warbler

May 27, 1853

Heard a stake driver [American bittern] yesterday in the rain. It sounded exactly like a man pumping while another man struck on the head of the pump with an axe—the last strokes sounding peculiarly dry and hard like a forcible echo from the woodside. One would think all Concord would be built on piles by this time. Very deliberately they drive and in the intervals are considering the progress of the pile into the soft mud. They are working by the day. He is early and late at his work, building his stadt-house—yet did anybody ever see the pile he had driven? He has come back from his southern tour to finish that job of spile driving which he undertook last year. It is heavy work—not to be hurried. Only green hands are overhasty.

American bittern

May 28, 1855

I see a tanager, the most brilliant and tropical looking bird we have—bright scarlet with black wings—the scarlet appearing on the rump again between wingtips. He brings heat—or heat him. A remarkable contrast with the green pines. At this distance he has the aspect and manners of a parrot—with a fullness about the head and throat and beak—indolently inspecting the limbs and twigs leaning over to it—and sitting still a long time. The female too is a neat and handsome bird—with the same indolent ways—but very differently colored from the male, all yellow below with merely dusky wings, and a sort of clay (?) color on back.

Scarlet tanager

May 29, 1855

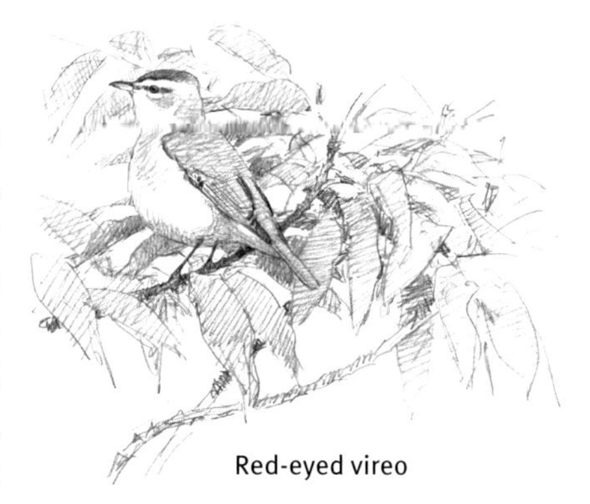
Red-eyed vireo

There are a great many birds now on the Island Neck. The red-eye [red-eyed vireo], its clear loud song in bars continuously repeated and varied—all tempered white beneath and dark yellow olive above and on edge of wings with a dark line on side-head or from root of bill—dusky claws—and a very long bill. The long bill—and the dark line on the side of the head with the white above and beneath or in the midst of the white, giving it a certain oblong swelled cheek look—would distinguish in a side view.

There is also the warbling vireo with its smooth flowing continuous one-barred shorter strain—with methinks a dusky side-head. Also the yellow-throated vireo. Its head and shoulders as well as throat yellow (apparently olive yellow above)—and its strain but little varied and short not continuous. It has dusky legs and two very distinct white bars on wings (the male).

May 30, 1852

Now is the summer come. A breezy washing day. A day for shadows—even of moving clouds over fields in which the grass is beginning to wave. Senecio in bloom. A bird's nest in grass with coffee-colored eggs.

May 31, 1855

Another *windy—washing day*—but warm. See a yellowbird building a nest on a white oak on the Island. She goes to a fern for the wool.

Yellow warbler and nest

JUNE

June 1, 1853

Walking up this sidehill—I disturbed a nighthawk eight or ten feet from me which went half fluttering half hopping. The mottled creature like a winged toad as Nuttall says the French of Louisiana (?) call them down the hill as far as I could see. Without moving I looked about and saw its two eggs on the bare ground on a slight shelf of the hill—on the dead pine needles and sand—without any cavity or nest whatever—very obvious when once you had detected them—but not easily detected from their color—a coarse gray formed of white spotted with a bluish or slaty brown or umber—a stone-granite color like the places it selects. I advanced and put my hand on them—and while I stooped seeing a shadow on the ground looked up and saw the bird which had fluttered down the hill so blind and helpless circling low and swiftly past over my head showing the white spot on each wing in true nighthawk fashion. When I had gone a dozen rods—it appeared again—higher in the air with its peculiar flitting limping kind of flight—all the while noiseless and suddenly descending it dashed at me within ten feet of my head like an imp of darkness—then swept away high over the pond dashing now to this side now to that on different tacks as if in pursuit of its prey it had already forgotten its eggs on the earth. I can see how it might easily come to be regarded with superstitious awe. A cuckoo very plainly heard.

Common nighthawk

June 2, 1859

Found within three rods of Flint's Pond a rose-breasted grosbeak's nest and one fresh egg (three on the 4th). It was in a thicket—where there was much catbriar—in a high blueberry bush—some five feet from the ground—in the forks of the bush—and of very loose construction—being made of the dead gray extremities of the catbriar with its tendrils (and some of this had dropped on the ground beneath) and this was lined—lined merely with fine brown stems of weeds like pinweeds—without any leaves or anything else—a slight nest on the whole. Saw the birds. The male uttered a very peculiar sharp clicking or squeaking note of alarm while I was near the nest.

The egg is thickly spotted with reddish brown on a pale blue ground (not white ground as Buonaparte and the New York ornithologist says) like a hermit thrush's but rounder—very delicate.

June 3, 1850

Returning I saw in Sudbury 25 nests of the new (cliff?) swallow under the eaves of a barn. They seemed particularly social and loquacious neighbors—though their voices are rather squeaking. Their nests built side by side looked somewhat like large hornets' nests, enough so to prove a sort of connection. Their activity, sociability and chattiness make them fit pensioners and neighbors of man—summer companions—for the barnyard.

Canada warbler

June 4, 1855

Great white-bosomed clouds darker beneath float through the cleared sky—and are seen against the deliciously blue sky—such a sky as we have not had before. Thus it is after the first important rain at this season. The song of birds is more lively and seems to have a new character—a new season has commenced. In the woods—I hear the tanager—and chewink—and red-eye. . . .

In the clintonia [blue-bead lily] swamp I hear a smart brisk loud and clear whistling warble—quite novel and remarkable—something like *te chit a wit, te chit a wit, tchit a wit, tche tche*. It is all bright yellow or ochreous *orange* (?) below except vent and a dark or black crescent on breast—with a white line about eye. Above it appears a nearly uniform dark blue slate, legs light, bill dark (?), tail long and forked. I think it must be the Canada warbler seen in '37 though that seems *short* for this. It is quite different from the warbler of May 30.

June 5, 1854

Now just before sundown a nighthawk is circling imp-like with undulating irregular flight over the sproutland on the Cliff Hill—with an occasional squeak and showing the spots on his wings. He does not circle away from this place—and I associate him with two gray eggs somewhere on the ground beneath—and a mate there sitting.

This squeak and occasional booming is heard in the evening air—while the stillness on the side of the village makes more distinct the increased hum of insects. I see at a distance a kingbird or blackbird pursuing a crow—lower down the hill—like a satellite revolving about a black planet. I have come to this hill to see the sun go down—to recover sanity and put myself again in relation with Nature.

June 6, 1857

As I sit on Lee's Cliff—I see a pe-pe [olive-sided flycatcher] on the topmost dead branch of a hickory eight or ten rods off. Regularly at short intervals it utters its monotonous note like *till-till-till*—or *pe-pe-pe*. Looking round for its prey and occasionally changing its perch, it every now and then darts off (phoebe-like) even five or six rods toward the east to catch an insect—and then returns to its favorite perch. If I lose it for a moment—I soon see it settling on the dead twigs again—and hear its *till, till, till*. It appears through the glass mouse-colored above—and head (which is perhaps darker), white throat and narrow white beneath—with no white on tail.

Olive-sided flycatcher

June 7, 1853

The ovenbird runs from her covered nest so close to the ground under the lowest twigs and leaves—even the loose leaves on the ground like a mouse that I cannot get a fair view of her—she does not fly at all. Is it to attract me, or partly to protect herself?

June 8, 1858

The marsh hawk's eggs are not yet hatched. She rises when I get within a rod—and utters that peculiar cackling or scolding note, much *like* but distinct from, that of the pigeon woodpecker. She keeps circling over the nest and repeatedly stoops within a rod of my head in an angry manner. She is not so large as a hen hawk—and is much more slender. She will come sailing swiftly and down over the tops of the trees and bushes etc. and then stoop as near to my head as she dares in order to scare me away. The primaries—of which I count but five—are very long and loose or distant like fingers—with which she takes hold of the air—and form a very distinct part of the wing—making an angle with the rest. Yet they are not broad—and give to the wing a long and slender appearance. The legs are stretched straight back under the tail. I see nothing of the male—nor did I before. A red-wing and a kingbird are soon in pursuit of the hawk—which proves, I think, that she meddles with their nests or themselves. She circles over me scolding, as far as the edge of the wood or 15 rods.

June 9, 1854

The air is now pretty full of shad flies—and there is an incessant sound made by the fishes leaping for such as are struggling on the surface—it sounds like the *lapsing* of a swift stream—sucking amid rocks. The fishes make a business of thus getting their evening meal—dimpling the river like large drops as far as I can see. Sometimes making a loud plashing. Meanwhile the kingfishers are on the lookout for the fishes as they rise and I saw one dive in the twilight and go off uttering his *cr-r-ack, cr-r-rack*.

Belted kingfisher

June 10, 1856

In a hollow apple tree—hole 18 inches deep—young pigeon woodpeckers—large and well feathered. They utter their squeaking hiss whenever I cover the hole with my hand apparently taking it for the approach of the mother. A strong rank fetid smell issues from the hole.

June 11, 1851

I hear the nighthawks uttering their squeaking notes high in the air now at nine o'clock P.M., and occasionally what I do not remember to have heard so late their booming note. It sounds more as if under a cope than by day. The sound is not so fugacious, going off to be lost amid the spheres, but is echoed hollowly to earth, making the low roof of heaven vibrate. Such a sound is more confused and dissipated by day.

June 12, 1853

The note of the wood thrush answers to some cool unexhausted morning vigor in the hearer. . . . Crows like hawks betray the neighborhood of their nests by harsh scolding at the intruder while they circle over the top of the wood. The red-eyed vireo is the bird most commonly heard in the woods. The wood thrush and the cuckoo also are heard now at noon. . . .

Going up Pine Hill—disturbed a partridge and her brood. She ran in deshabille directly to me—within four feet—while her young, not larger than a chicken just hatched, dispersed flying along a foot or two from the ground just over the bushes for a rod or two. The mother kept close at hand to attract my attention, and mewed and clucked and made a noise as when a hawk is in sight. She stepped about and held her head above the bushes and clucked just like a hen. What a remarkable instinct that which keeps the young so silent—and prevents their peeping and betraying themselves. This wild bird will run almost any risk to save her young. The young I believe make a fine sound at first in dispersing—something like a cherry bird. . . .

I forgot to say that I visited my hawk's nest and the young hawk was perched now four or five feet above the nest. Still in the shade. It will soon fly. Now there in secluded pine woods the young hawks sit high on the edges of their nests or on the twigs nearby in the shade—waiting for their pinions to grow. While their parents bring to them their prey. Their silence also is remarkable. Not to betray themselves—nor will the old bird go to the nest while you are in sight. She pursues me half a mile when I withdraw.

June 13, 1853

9 A.M. to Orchis Swamp. Find that there are two young hawks. One has left the nest and is perched on a small maple seven or eight rods distant. This one appears much smaller than the former one. I am struck by its large naked head so vulture-like—and large eyes—as if the vulture's was an inferior stage through which the hawk passed. Its feet too are large—remarkably developed—by which it holds to its perch securely like an old bird, before its wings can perform their office. It has a buff breast striped with dark brown. Pratt, when I told him of this nest, said he would like to carry one of his rifles down there. But I told him that I should be sorry to have them killed. I would rather save one of these hawks than have a hundred hens and chickens. It was worth more to see them soar—especially now that they are so rare in the landscape. It is easy to buy eggs—but not to buy hen hawks. My neighbors would not hesitate to shoot the last pair of hen hawks in the town to save a few of their chickens! But such economy is narrow and groveling. It is unnecessary to sacrifice the greater value to the less. I would rather never taste chicken's meat—nor hen's eggs—than never to see a hawk sailing through the upper air again. This sight is worth incomparably more than a chicken soup or a boiled egg. So we exterminate the deer, and substitute the hog. It was amusing to observe the swaying to and fro of the young hawk's head to counterbalance the gentle motion of the bough in the wind.

Young red-tailed hawk

June 14, 1851

Upland sandpiper

I could go about the world listening for the strains of music. Men use this gift but sparingly methinks. What should we think of a bird which had the gift of song but used it only once in a dozen years! Like the tree which blossoms only once in a century.

June 15, 1860

After proceeding half a dozen rods toward the hill I heard the familiar willet note of the upland plover [upland sandpiper]—and looking up saw one standing erect (like a large telltale [greater yellowlegs]—or chicken with its head stretched up) on the rail fence. After a while it flew off southwest and low then wheeled and went a little higher down the river. Of pigeon size—but quick quivering wings. Finally rose higher and flew more or less zigzag as if uncertain where it would alight—and at last when almost out of sight it pitched down into a field near Cyrus Hubbard's. It was the same note I heard so well on Cape Cod in July '55—and *probably* the same I heard in the Shawsheen valley May 15, '58. I suspect then that it breeds here.

June 16, 1853

Virginia rail

Coming down the river heard opposite the new houses where I stopped to pluck the tall grass—a sound as of young blackbirds amid the buttonbushes. After a long while gazing—standing on the roots of the buttonbushes I detected a couple of meadow or mud hens [Virginia rail], *Rallus virginianus*, gliding about under the buttonbushes over the mud and through the shallow water and uttering a squeaking or squawking note as if they had a nest there or young. Bodies about the size of a robin—short tail—wings and tail white-edged—bill about one and a half inches long—orange beneath in one bird. Brown deepening into black spots above. Turtle dove color on breasts and beneath. Ashy about eyes and cheeks. Seemed not willing to fly—and for a long time unwilling to pass me—because it must come near to keep under the buttonbushes.

Black-throated green warbler

June 17, 1854

The evergreen forest bird at old place on white pine and oak tops—top of Brister's Hill on right—I think it has black wings with white bars. Is it not the black-throated green warbler?

June 18, 1854

Examined as well as I could with the glass what I will call the tweezer bird [northern parula],—*tra-wee, shreea-shre*—raspingly. I have heard [it] perhaps as long as the evergreen forest. It is a slender, somewhat small vireo-like bird—yellow and yellowish all beneath—except a chestnutish (?) crescent on breast—with apparently a white spot on the wing—and certainly a yellow or greenish yellow back between wings. Keeping rather high in the trees—I could not see the general color of the upper parts but thought it was dark olivaceous or maybe slaty. Can it be the blue yellow-back warbler?

Northern parula

June 19, 1853

The air is full of the hum of invisible insects—and I hear a locust. Perhaps this sound indicates the time to put on a thin coat. But the wood thrush sings as usual far in the wood. A blue jay and a tanager come dashing into the pine under which I stand. The first flies directly away screaming with suspicion or disgust—but the latter more innocent remains. The cuckoo is heard too in the depths of the wood.

June 20, 1856

Walking under an apple tree in the little Baker Farm peach orchard—heard an incessant shrill musical twitter or peeping as from young birds over my head—and looking up saw a hole in an upright dead bough some 15 feet from ground. Climbed up and finding that the shrill twitter came from it—guessed it to be the nest of a downy woodpecker—which proved to be the case—for it reminded me of the hissing squeak or squeaking hiss of young pigeon woodpeckers—but this was more musical or bird-like. The bough was about 4½ inches in diameter—and the hole *perfectly circular* about 1¼ inch in diameter. Apparently nests had been in holes above now broken out—higher up. When I put my fingers in it the young breathed their shrill twitter louder than ever. Anon the old appeared and came quite near while I stood in the tree keeping up an incessant loud and shrill scolding note and also after I descended—not to be relieved.

June 21, 1853

The nest of a brown thrasher with three eggs on some greenbriar perfectly concealed by a grape vine running over it—eggs greenish brown—nest of dry sticks—lined with fibers of grape bark and with roots. Bird scolded me much. . . .

Where the other day I saw a pigeon woodpecker tapping and enlarging a hole in the dead limb of an apple tree—when as yet probably no egg was laid, today I see two well-grown young woodpeckers about as big as the old, looking out at the hole showing their handsome spotted breasts and calling lustily for something to eat—or it may be suffering from the heat. Young birds in some situations must suffer greatly from heat these days—so closely packed in their nests and perhaps insufficiently shaded. It is a wonder they remain so long there patiently. I saw a yellowbird's nest in the willows on the causeway this P.M. and three young birds nearly ready to fly overflowing the nest—all holding up their open bills and keeping them steadily open for a minute or more on noise of my approach. Still see cherry birds in flocks.

June 22, 1851

Still the blackberries love to creep over this floor, for it is not many years since this was a blackberry field. And I hear around me but never in sight the many wood thrushes—whetting their steel-like notes. Such keen singers. It takes a fiery heat—many dry pine leaves added to the furnace of the sun to temper their strains. Always they are either rising or falling to a new strain. After what a moderate pause they deliver themselves again saying ever a new thing—avoiding repetition. Methinks answering one another. While most other birds take their siesta—the wood thrush discharges his song.

June 23, 1851

It is a pleasant sound to me, the squeaking and the booming of nighthawks flying over high open fields in the woods. They fly like butterflies not to avoid birds of prey but apparently to secure their own insect prey. There is a particular part of the railroad just below the shanty where they may be heard and seen in greatest numbers. But often you must look a long while before you can detect the mote in the sky from which the note proceeds.

June 24, 1853

The brown thrasher's nest . . . has been robbed probably by some other bird. It rested on a branch of a swamp pink and some grape vines—effectually concealed and protected by grape vines and greenbriar in a matted bower above it. The foundation of pretty stout twigs eight or nine inches in diameter surmounted by coarse strips of grape bark giving form to the nest—and then lined with some harsh wiry root-fibers within rather small and shallow—and the whole fabric of loose texture not easy to remove.

Nighthawks

Also got a [red-winged] blackbird's nest whose inhabitants had flown. Hung by a kind of small dried rush (?) between two buttonbushes which crossed above it— of meadow grass and sedge—dried *Mikania scandens* [climbing hempweed] vine—horsetail—fish lines—and a strip apparently of a lady's bathing dress—lined with a somewhat finer grass—of a loose and ragged texture to look at. Green mikania running over it now.

A yellowbird's nest . . . in a fork of a willow on Hubbard's Causeway—resting chiefly on the leading branch—of fine grass lined with hair, bottom outside puffing out with a fine light flax-like fiber, perhaps the bark of some weed—by which also it is fastened to the twigs. It is surprising that so many birds find hair enough to line their nests with. If I wish for a horsehair for my compass sights I must go to the stable—but the hairbird, with her sharp eyes, goes to the road.

June 25, 1852

I observe that young birds are usually of a duller color and more speckled than old ones—as if for their protection in their tender state. They have not yet the markings (and the beauty) which distinguish their species—and which betray it often—but by their colors are merged in the variety of colors of the season.

June 26, 1855

C. [Ellery Channing] has found a wood pewee's nest on a horizontal limb of a small swamp white oak ten feet high with three fresh eggs cream colored with spots of two shades in a ring about large end. Have nest and an egg.

June 27, 1852

I meet the partridge with her brood in the woods—a perfect little hen. She spreads her tail into a fan and beats the ground with her wings fearlessly within a few feet of me to attract my attention while her young disperse— but they keep up a faint wiry kind of peep—which betrays them—while she mews and squeaks as if giving them directions.

June 28, 1857

I hear on all hands these days—from the elms and other trees—the twittering peep of young gold robins [Baltimore orioles]—which have recently left their nests, and apparently indicate their locality to their parents by thus incessantly peeping all day long.

Baltimore oriole

Chestnut-sided warbler

June 29, 1859

At the railroad spring in Howard's meadow, I see two chestnut-sided warblers—hopping and skipping as if they had a nest within six feet of me a long time. No doubt they are breeding near. Yellow crown with a fine dark longitudinal line—reddish chestnut sides—black triangle on side of head—white beneath.

June 30, 1851

The cuckoo is faintly heard from a neighboring grove. Now that it is beginning to be dark, as I am crossing a pasture I hear a happy cricket-like—shrill little lay—from a sparrow either in the grass or else on that distant tree—as if it were the vibrations of a watch spring—its vespers....

Saw a brood of young partridges yesterday a little larger than robins.

Black-billed cuckoo

JULY

July 1, 1860

While reclining on the sedge at end of townbound path . . . I see a warbler deliberately investigating the smooth sumac, and their old berry bunches—in various positions. It is a slaty blue above—with a bright yellow front head—and much yellow on the wings at angle, etc.—a very distinct black throat triangularwise with a broad black line through the eyes on side head—a forked tail which is dark beneath—belly and vent white or whitish.

It is undoubtedly the *Sylvia chrysoptera* or golden-winged warbler which I think must be breeding here.

July 2, 1853

I hear a harsh *keow* from a bittern flying over the river. The peetweets are quite noisy about the rocks in Merrick's pasture when I approach. Have eggs or young there—which they are anxious about.

Spotted sandpiper

Black ducks

July 3, 1857

Minott says that old Joe Merriam used to tell of his shooting black ducks in the Dam Meadows—and what luck he had. One day he had shot a couple of ducks and was bringing them home by the legs, when he came to a ditch. As he had his gun in the other hand, and the ditch was wide, he thought he would toss the ducks over before he jumped—but they had no sooner struck the ground than they picked themselves up and flew away—which discouraged him with respect to duck-shooting.

July 4, 1852

A [ruby-throated] hummingbird hums by over the pads up the river as if looking like myself to see if lilies have blossomed.

Ruby-throated hummingbird

July 5, 1852

Some birds are poets and sing all summer—they are the true singers. Any man can write verses during the love season. I am reminded of this while we rest in the shade on the Major Heywood road—and listen to a wood thrush now just before sunset. We are most interested in those birds who sing for the love of the music and not of their mates—who meditate their strains and *amuse* themselves with singing. The birds—the strains of deeper sentiment—not bobolinks that lose their plumage, their bright colors and their song so early. . . .

The wood thrush's is no opera music—it is not so much the composition as the strain, the tone—cool bars of melody from the atmospheres of everlasting morning or evening. It is the quality of the song not the sequence. In the peawai's [eastern wood pewee] note there is

Wood thrush

some sultriness—but in the thrush's, though heard at noon, there is the liquid coolness of things that are just drawn from the bottom of springs. The thrush alone declares the immortal wealth and vigor that is in the forest. Here is a bird in whose strain the story is told—though Nature waited for the science of aesthetics to discover it to man. Whenever a man hears it he is young—and nature is in her spring. Wherever he hears it it is a new world—and a free country—and the gates of heaven are not shut against him. Most other birds sing from the level of my ordinary cheerful hours—a carol—but this bird never fails to speak to me out of an ether purer than that I breathe—of immortal beauty and vigor. He deepens the significance of all things seen in the light of his strain. He sings to make men take higher and truer views of things. He sings to amend their institutions. To relieve the slave on the plantation—and the prisoner in his dungeon—the slave in the house of luxury and the prisoner of his own low thoughts. . . .

I hear my hooting owl [great horned owl] now just before sunset. You can fancy it the most melancholy sound in nature, as if Nature meant by this to stereotype and make permanent in her quire the dying moans of a human being—made more awful by a certain gurgling melodiousness. It reminds of ghouls—and idiots—and insane howlings. One answers from far woods in a strain made really sweet by distance. Some poor weak relic of mortality who has left hope behind, and howls like an animal—yet with human sobs—on entering the dark valley. I find myself beginning with the letters *gl* when I try to imitate it. Yet for the most part it is a sweet and melodious strain to me.

July 6, 1852

A quail. I associate its whistle with breezy weather.

July 7, 1852

The fog condenses into fountains and streams of music as in the strain of the bobolink which I hear—and runs off so. The music of the birds is the tinkling of the rills that flow from it.

Bobolinks

July 8, 1854

The whippoorwills are heard and the baying of dogs.

July 9, 1860

See two handsome rose-breasted grosbeaks on the Corner causeway. One utters a peculiar squeaking or snapping note—and both by form of bill and this note reminds me of some of those foreign birds with great bills in cages.

There is a smart shower at 5 P.M. and in the midst of it a hummingbird is busy about the flowers in the garden—unmindful of it—though you would think that each big drop that struck him would be a serious accident.

July 10, 1851

A gorgeous sunset after rain with horizontal bars of clouds, red sashes to the western window—barry clouds hanging like a curtain over the window of the west—damask. . . . How many times I have seen this kind of sunset—the most gorgeous sight in nature. From the hill behind Minott's I see the birds flying against this red sky, the sun having set—one looks like a bat. . . .

A softer amber sky than in any picture. The swallows are improving this short day—twittering as they fly, and the huckleberry bird [field sparrow] repeats his jingling strain—and the song sparrow more honest than most. . . .

And the nighthawk dashes past in the twilight with mottled (?) wing within a rod of me.

July 11, 1857

Haying is fairly begun—and for some days I have heard the sound of the mowing machine—and now the lark must look out for the mowers.

July 12, 1852

I observed this morning a row of several dozen swallows perched on the telegraph wire by the bridge—and ever and anon a part of them would launch forth as with one consent—circle a few moments over the water or meadow and return to the wire again. . . .

The kingbird is active over the causeway notwithstanding the heat. And near the woods I hear the huckleberry bird—and the song sparrow.

Brown-headed cowbirds

July 13, 1856

In Hubbard's euphorbia pasture cow blackbirds about cows. At first the cows were resting and ruminating in the shade and no birds were seen. Then one after another got up and went to feeding—straggling into the midst of the field. With a chattering appeared a cowbird and with a long slanting flight lit close to a cow's nose within the shadow of it—and watched for insects—the cow still eating along and almost hitting it—taking no notice of it. Soon it is joined by two or three more birds.

July 14, 1856

While drinking at Assabet Spring in woods—noticed a cherry stone on the bottom. A bird that came to drink must have brought it—half a mile. So the tree gets planted!

July 15, 1854

This cooler, still cloudy weather after the rain is very autumnal and restorative to our spirits. The robin sings—still—but the goldfinch twitters over oftener—and I hear the *link link* of the bobolink (one perfect strain!) and the crickets creak more as in the fall. All these sounds dispose our minds to serenity. . . .

I hear a baywing on the wall nearby sound far away—a fainter song sparrow strain somewhat. I see its open mouth and quivering throat yet can hardly believe the seemingly distant strain proceeds from it—*yaw yaw / twee twee / twitter twitter—te twee twe tw tw tw* and so ends with a short and rapid trill.

July 16, 1854

Savannah sparrow

Many yellow butterflies and red on clover and yarrow. Is it the yellow-winged or Savannah sparrow with yellow alternating with dark streaks on throat—as well as yellow over eye—reddish flesh-colored legs and two light bars on wings?

July 17, 1856

A very warm afternoon. Thermometer at 97° at the Hosmer Desert. I hear the early locust. I have come to collect birds' nests. The thrasher's is apparently made partly beneath the surface, some dirt making its sides. I find the nests by withered twigs and leaves broken off in the spring, but commonly nearly concealed by the recent growth. The jay's nest had been filled with white oak leaves. Not one could have been blown into it.

July 18, 1852

We take a bath at Hubbard's Bend. The water seems fresher as the air in the morning. Again under weigh we scare up the great bittern amid the pontederia [pickerelweed]—and rowing to where he alights come within three feet of him and scare him up again. He flies sluggishly away plowing the air with the coulter of his breastbone and alighting ever higher up the stream. We scare him up many times in the course of an hour.

July 19, 1860

Minott who sits alone confined to his room with dropsy—observed the other day that it was a cold summer. He knew it was cold—the whip-poorwill told him so. It sung once and then stopped.

July 20, 1852

The pitch pine woods are heavy and dark—but the river is full of golden light—and more conspicuous than by day. It is starlight—you see the first star in the southwest and know not how much earlier you might have seen it had you looked. Now the first whippoorwill sings hollowly in the dark pitch pine wood on Bear Garden Hill—as if the night had never ceased and it had never ceased to sing—only now we heard it. And now when we had thought the day birds gone to roost—the wood thrush takes up the strain—the bullfrog trumps.

July 21, 1856

These hot afternoons I go panting through the close sproutlands and copses—as now from Cliff Brook to Wheeler Meadow—and occasionally come to sandy places a few feet in diameter where the partridges have dusted themselves. Gerard the Lion Killer of Algiers speaks of seeing similar spots when tracking or patiently waiting the lion there and his truth in this particular is a confirmation of the rest of his story. But his pursuit dwarfs this fact and makes it seem trivial. Shall not my pursuit also contrast with the trivialness of the partridge's dusting? It is interesting to find that the same phenomena, however simple, occur in different parts of the globe. I have found an arrowhead or two in such places even. Far in warm sandy woods in hot weather—when not a breath of air is stirring—I come upon these still sandier and warmer spots where the partridges have dusted themselves—now all still and deserted—and am not relieved yet pleased to find that I have been preceded by any creature.

July 22, 1852

This morning though perfectly fair except a haziness in the east which prevented any splendor—the birds do not sing as yesterday. They appear to make distinctions which we cannot appreciate, and perhaps sing with most animation on the finest mornings.

Flocks of yellow-breasted russet-backed female bobolinks are seen flitting stragglingly across the meadows. The bobolink loses his song as he loses his colors.

July 23, 1851

The swallow's twitter is the sound of the lapsing waves of the air—or when they break and burst—as his wings represent the ripple. He has more air in his bones than other birds—his feet are defective—the fish of the air—his note is the voice of the air. As fishes may hear the sound of waves lapsing on the surface and see the outlines of the ripples so we hear the note and see the flight of swallows.

Northern bobwhite

July 24, 1852

The cardinal flower probably open today. The quails are heard whistling this morning near the village. . . .

I heard this afternoon the cool water twitter of the goldfinch and saw the bird. They come with the springing aftermath. It is refreshing as a cup of cold water to a thirsty man to hear them, now only one at a time.

July 25, 1852

4 A.M. To Cliffs. This early twitter or breathing of chip-birds in the dawn sounds like something organic in the earth. This is a morning celebrated by birds. Our bluebird sits on the peak of the house and warbles as in the spring—but as he does not now by day.

Chipping sparrow

July 26, 1853

The bobolinks are just beginning to fly in flocks and I hear their *link link*. I see the young birds also just able to get out of my way above the weeds and bushes of the low grounds, their tails not grown out to steady them. Larks too seen now four or five together—and sing as of yore. Also the goldfinch twitters over oftener.

July 27, 1852

How cool and assuaging the thrush's note after the fever of the day. I doubt if they have anything so richly wild in Europe. So long a civilization must have banished it. It will only be heard in America perchance while our star is in the ascendant. I should be very much surprised if I were to hear in the strain of the nightingale such unexplored wildness and fertility reaching to sundown—inciting to emigration.

July 28, 1859

The sweet and plaintive note of the pewee (wood pewee) is now prominent, since most other birds are more hushed.

I hear probably young families of them answering each other from a considerable distance especially about the river. Hear also part of the song of what sounds and looks like a rose-breasted grosbeak. Saw young martins being fed on a bridge rail yesterday.

July 29, 1856

Pratt says he one day walked out with Wesson with their rifles—as far as Hunt's Bridge. Looking downstream he saw a swallow sitting on a bush very far off—at which he took aim and fired with ball. He was surprised to see that he had touched the swallow for it flew directly across the river toward Simon Brown's barn—always descending toward the earth or water—not being able to maintain itself—but what surprised him most was to see a second swallow come flying behind and repeated strike the other with all his force beneath so as to toss him up as often as he approached the ground and enable him to continue his flight—and thus he continued to do till they were out of sight. Pratt said he resolved that he would never fire at a swallow again.

July 30, 1852

How long is it since I heard a veery? Do they go or become silent when the goldfinch heralds the autumn? Do not all flowers that blossom after mid-July remind us of the fall? After midsummer we have a belated feeling as if we had all been idlers—and are forward to see in each sight—and hear in each sound some presage of the fall. Just as in middle age man anticipates the end of life. Tansy is a prevalent flower now—dogsbane still common. Nighthawks squeak and fly low over Thrush Alley at 4 P.M.

Eastern wood pewee

July 31, 1858

Got the wood thrushes' nest of June 19 (now empty). It was placed between many small upright shoots—against the main stem of the slender maple, and measures 4½ to 5 inches in diameter from outside to outside of the rim and 1¾ deep within. It is quite firm (except the external leaves falling off) the rim about ¾ of an inch thick—and it is composed externally of leaves, of chiefly chestnut—very much decayed—beneath which, in the place of the grass and stubble of which most nests are composed—are apparently the midribs of the same leaves—whose whole pulp etc. is gone—arranged as compactly and densely (in a curving manner)—as grass or stubble could be—upon a core, not of mud, but a pale brown composition quite firm and smooth within looking like made of a cocoanut shell—and apparently composed of decayed leaf pulp (?) which the bird has perhaps mixed and cemented with its saliva. This is about ¼ of an inch thick—and about as regular as half of a cocoanut shell. Within this the lower part is lined with considerable rather coarse black root fiber and a very little fine stubble.

Veery

From some particles of fine white sand etc. on the pale brown composition of the nest—I thought it was obtained from the pond shore. This composition viewed through a microscope has almost a cellular structure.

AUGUST

Green heron

August 1, 1858

Ed. Bartlett and another brought me a green bittern [green heron], this year's first, apparently—full grown but not full plumaged—which they caught near the pool on A. Heywood's land behind Sleepy Hollow. They caught it in the woods on the hillside. It had not yet acquired the long feathers of the neck.

The neck was bent back on itself an inch or more that part being bare of feathers and covered by the long feathers from above, so that it did not appear very long—until stretched out. This doubling was the usual condition and not apparent—but could be felt by the hand. So the green bitterns are leaving the nest now.

August 2, 1854

The surface of the forest on the east of the river presents a singularly cool and wild appearance—cool as a pot of green paint—stretches of green light and shade—reminding me of some lonely mountainside. The nighthawk flies low—skimming over the ground now.

August 3, 1859

I see two or three birds which I take to be rose-breasted grosbeaks of this year. They are speckled brown and white (with considerable white) birds, and no rose on breast that I see. I hear them singing a little in a grosbeak-like strain—but a more partial warble. Heard one July 28 on an oak high up Assabet—and today on an apple tree near Brister's.

August 4, 1855

Just after bathing at the rock near the Island this P.M.—after sunset—I saw a flock of thousands of barn swallows and some white-bellied [tree swallow] and perhaps others, for it was too dark to distinguish them. They came flying over the river in loose array—wheeled and flew round in a great circle over the bay there about 80 feet high with a loud twittering as if seeking a resting place—then flew up the stream. I was very much surprised at their numbers. Directly after, hearing a buzzing sound we found them all alighted on the dense golden willow hedge at Shattuck's shore—parallel with the shore—quite densely leaved and 18 feet high. They were generally perched five or six feet from the top amid the thick leaves—filling it for eight or ten rods. They were very restless fluttering from one perch to another and about one another—and kept up a loud and remarkable buzzing or squeaking—breathing or hum—with only occasionally a regular twitter—now and then flitting alongside from one end of the row to the other. It was so dark we had to draw close to see them.

Barn swallow in flight

At intervals they were perfectly still for a moment—as if at a signal. At length after 20 or 30 minutes of bustle and hum—they all settled quietly to rest on their perches—I supposed for the night. We had rowed up within a rod of one end of the row—looking up so as to bring the birds between us and the sky—but they paid not the slightest attention to us. What was remarkable was first their numbers—second their perching on densely leaved willows—third their buzzing or humming like a hive of bees—even squeaking notes—and fourth their disregarding our nearness. I supposed that they were preparing to migrate—being the early broods.

August 5, 1858

[Black willows on the riverbanks] resound still with the sprightly twitter of the kingbird—that aerial and spirited bird hovering over them—swallow-like—which likes best methinks to fly where the sky is reflected beneath him.... The kingbird by his activity and lively note and his white breast keeps the air sweet. He sits now on a dead willow twig—akin to the flecks of mackerel sky—with reflections in the water—or the white clamshell wrong side out opened by a musquash—or the fine particles of white quartz that may be found in the muddy river's sand. He is here to give a voice to all these. The willow's dead twig is aerial perch enough for him. Even the swallows deign to perch on it....

Marsh wren

Just opposite this bay [Lily Bay, Sudbury] I heard a peculiar note which I thought at first might be that of a kingbird—but soon saw for the first time a wren within two or three rods perched on the tall sedge or the woolgrass and making it—probably the short-billed marsh wren. It was peculiarly brisk and rasping—not at all musical—the rhythm something like *shar te dittle ittle ittle ittle ittle*. But the last part was drier or less liquid than this implies. It was a small bird quite dark above, and apparently plain ashy white beneath—and held its head up when it sang—and also commonly its tail. It dropped into the deep sedge on our approach—but did not go off as we saw by the motion of the grass. Then stopped and uttered its brisk notes quite near us—and flying off was lost in the sedge again.

August 6, 1852

How different the feeble twittering of the birds here at sunrise from the full quire of the spring. Only the wood thrush, a huckleberry bird or two, or chickadee—the scream of a flicker or a jay—or the caw of a crow—and commonly only an alarmed note of a robin. A solitary peawai may be heard perchance—or a red-eye. But no thrashers—or catbirds—or ovenbirds—or the jingle of the chewink. I hear the ominous twittering of the goldfinch over all. . . .

Summer gets to be an old story. Birds leave off singing, as flowers blossoming—i.e. perhaps in the same proportion. With the goldenrod comes the goldfinch. About the time his cool twitter was heard, did not the bobolink—thrasher—catbird—ovenbird—veery etc. cease?

August 7, 1858

But not these sights alone are now seen on the river—but the sprightly kingbird glances and twitters above the glossy leaves of the swamp white oak. Perchance this tree—with its leaves glossy above—whitish beneath—best expresses the *life* of the kingbird—and is its own tree.

Eastern kingbird

August 8, 1858

Grasshopper sparrow

I see at Clamshell Hill—a yellow-browed sparrow [grasshopper sparrow] sitting quite near on a hay cock—pluming itself. Observe it a long time in all positions with my glass within two rods. It is probably a this year's bird. I think it must be the *F. passerina* for its breast and beneath is the clear pale ochreous white which Wilson speaks of—and its wing shoulder is distinctly yellow when not concealed in the feathers of the side. Its legs and bill except the upper side of the upper mandible are quite a reddish flesh color. The yellow on its temple is quite bright and the pale brownish cheeks. The crown is blackish with a distinct white line along the midst. I see what I call chestnut with the black and whitish on the back and wings. It stands very upright so that I can see all beneath. It utters no note i.e. song—only a faint short somewhat cricket-like or trilled chip.

August 9, 1853

You hear the peculiar scream of young hawks nowadays. The marsh hawks reddish beneath—which have not their perfect plumage.

August 10, 1854

There is a peculiar and distinct hollow sound made by the pigeon woodpecker's wings as it flies past near you. . . .

The tinkling notes of goldfinches and bobolinks which we hear nowadays are of one character—and peculiar to the season. They are not voluminous flowers—but rather nuts of sound. Ripened seeds of sound. It is the tinkling of ripened grains in Nature's basket. It is like the sparkle on water—a sound produced by friction on the crisped air.

August 11, 1858

Heard a fine sprightly richly warbled strain—from a bird perched on the top of a beanpole. It was at the same time novel yet familiar to me. I soon recognized it for the strain of the purple finch, which I have not heard lately. But though it appeared as large, it seemed a different colored bird. With my glass—four rods off—I saw it to be a goldfinch. It kept repeating this warble of the purple finch for several minutes. A very surprising note to be heard now when birds generally are so silent. Have not heard the purple finch of late. I conclude that the goldfinch is a very fine and powerful singer—and the most successful and remarkable mockingbird that we have. In the spring I heard it imitate the thrasher exactly—before that bird had arrived—and now it imitates the purple finch as perfectly—after the latter bird has ceased to sing! It is a surprising vocalist. It did not cease singing till I disturbed it by my nearer approach—and then it went off with its usual *mew* succeeded by its watery twitter in its *ricochet* flight.

August 12, 1851

There was a whippoorwill in the road just beyond Goodwin's which flew up and lighted on the fence and kept alighting on the fence within a rod of me and circling round me with a slight squeak as if inquisitive about me. . . .

Whippoorwill

(Not far from four still in the night I heard a nighthawk squeak and *boom* high in the air—as I sat on the cliff. What is said about this being less of a night bird than the whippoorwill is perhaps to be questioned. For neither do I remember to have heard the whippoorwill sing at 12 o'clock—though I met one sitting and flying between two and three this morning—I believe that both may be heard at midnight, though very rarely.)

Now at *very earliest* dawn the nighthawk booms and the whippoorwill sings. . . .

The birds utter a few languid and yawning notes as if they had not left their perches—so sensible to light to wake so soon. A faint peeping sound from I know not what kind—a slight innocent half-awake sound—like the sounds which a quiet housewife makes in the earliest dawn. Nature preserves her innocence like a beautiful child. I hear a wood thrush even now long before sunrise as in the heat of the day. And the pewee and the catbird—and the vireo—red-eyed?

I do not hear—or do not mind perchance—the crickets now. Now whippoorwills commence to sing in earnest considerably *after* the wood thrush. The wood thrush that beautiful singer inviting the day once more to enter his pine woods. (So you may hear the wood thrush and whippoorwill at the same time.) Now go by two whippoorwills in haste seeking some coverts from the eye of day. And the bats are flying about on the edge of the wood improving the last moments of their day in catching insects. The moon appears at length—not yet as a cloud—but with a frozen light ominous of her fate. The early cars sound like a wind in the woods. The chewinks make a business now of waking each other up with their low "*yorrick*" in the neighboring low copse.

August 13, 1858

I come to get the now empty nests of the wood pewees found June 27th. In each case—on approaching the spot I hear the sweet note of a pewee—lingering about—and this alone would have guided me within four or five rods. I do not know why they should linger near the empty nests but perhaps they have built again near there—or intend to use the same nest again (?). Their full strain is *pe-ah-ée* (perhaps repeated) rising on the last syllable and emphasizing that—then *pe'-ee*, emphasizing the first and falling on the last—all very sweet and rather plaintive suggesting innocence and confidence in you. In *this* case the bird uttered only its last strain—regularly at intervals.

These two pewee nests are remarkably alike in their position and composition and form—though half a mile apart. They are both placed on a horizontal branch of a young oak (one about 14—the other about 18 feet from ground) and three to five feet from main trunk in a young oak wood. Both rest directly on a horizontal fork—and such is their form and composition that they have almost precisely the same color and aspect from below—and from above.

August 14, 1859

When I reached the upper end of this weedy bar—at about 3 P.M. this warm day I noticed some light-colored object in midriver near the other end of the bar. At first I thought of some large stake or board standing amid the weeds there.... But about this time I discovered with my naked eye that it was a blue heron standing in very shallow water amid the weeds of the bar—and pluming itself.... I floated to within 25 rods and watched it at my leisure.

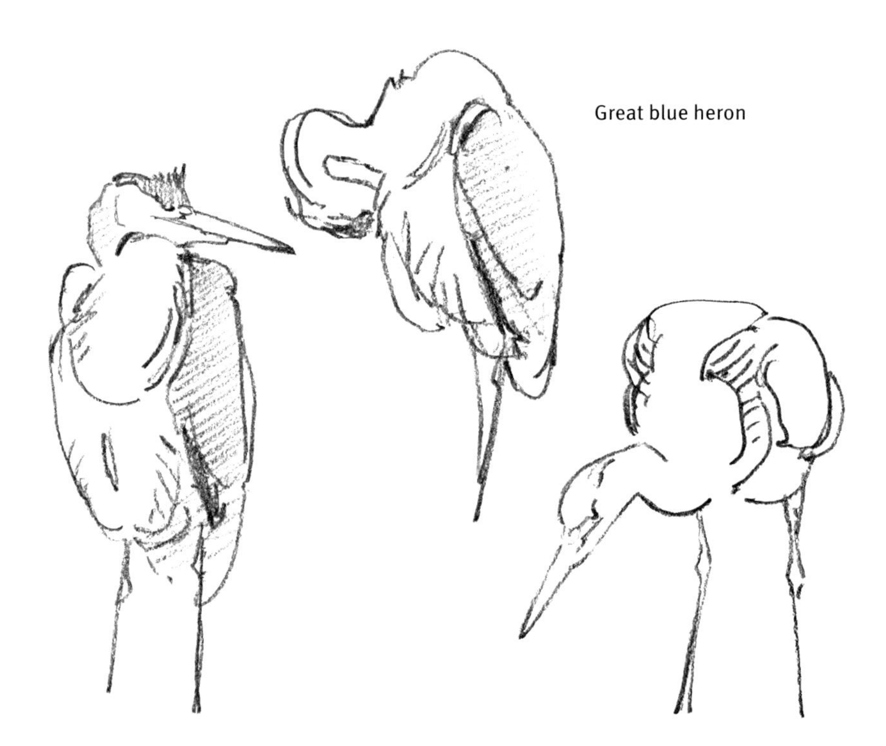

Great blue heron

Standing on the shallowest part of the bar at that end—it was busily dressing its feathers—passing its bill like a comb down its feathers from base to tip. From its form and color—as well as size, it was singularly distinct. Its great spear-shaped head and bill was very conspicuous, though least so when turned toward me (whom it was eyeing from time to time). It coils its neck away upon its back or breast as a sailor might a rope—but occasionally stretches itself to its full height as tall as a man and looks around—and at me. Growing shy it begins to wade off—until its body is partly immersed amid the weeds—potamogeton—and then it looks more like a goose. The neck is continually varying in length as it is doubled up or stretched out and the legs also, as it wades in deeper or shallower water.

Suddenly comes a second, flying low, and alights on the bar yet nearer to me—almost high and dry. Then I hear a note from them perhaps of warning—a *short* coarse frog-like purring or eructating sound. You might easily mistake it for a frog. I heard it half a dozen times. It was not very loud. Anything but musical. The last proceeds to plume himself, looking warily at me from time to time, while the other continues to edge off through the weeds. Now and then the latter holds its neck as if it were ready to strike its prey—stretched forward over the water—but I saw no stroke. The arch may be lengthened or shortened—single or double—but the great spear-shaped bill and head are ever the same. A great hammer or pick prepared to transfix fish, frog—or bird.

At last, the water becoming too deep for wading, this one takes easily to wing (though up to his body in water) and flies a few rods to the shore. It rather flies then than swims. It was evidently scared.

These were probably birds of this season. I saw some distinct ferruginous on the angle of the wing. There they stand in the midst of the open river—on this shallow and weedy bar in the sun. The leisurely sentries—lazily pluming themselves—as if the day were too long for them. They gave a new character to the stream. Adjutant they were to my idea of the river—these two winged men.

You have not seen our weedy river—you do not know the significance of its weedy bars—until you have seen the blue heron wading and pluming itself on it. I see that it was made for these shallows and they for it. Now the heron is gone from the weedy shoal the scene appears incomplete. Of course the heron has sounded the depth of the water on every bar of the river that is fordable to it. The water there is not so many feet deep—but so many heron's tibia. Instead of a foot rule you should use a heron's leg for a measure. If you would know the depth of the water on these few shoalest places of Musketaquid—ask the blue heron that wades and fishes there. In some places a heron can wade across.

August 15, 1854

Some birds, after they have ceased to sing by day continue to sing faintly in the morning now as in spring. I hear now a warbling vireo—a robin half strain—a golden robin whistles—bluebirds warble—pigeon woodpecker, not to mention the tapping of a woodpecker and the notes of birds which are heard through the day—as wood peawai—song sparrow—cuckoo etc. On the top of the hill I see the goldfinch eating the seeds (?) of the Canada thistle. I rarely approach a bed of them or other thistles nowadays but I hear the cool twitter of the goldfinch about it.

August 16, 1858

Channing tells me that he saw a white bobolink in a large flock of them today. Almost all flowers and animals may be found white. As in a large number of cardinal flowers you may find a white one—so in a large flock of bobolinks also, it seems, you may find a white one.

Tree swallow

August 17, 1851

The swallows skim low over the pastures twittering as they fly near me with forked tail dashing near me as if I scared up insects for them.

August 18, 1858

I sit under the oaks at the east end of Hubbard's Grove—and hear two wood pewees singing close by. They are perched on dead oak twigs four or five rods apart—and their notes are so exactly alike that at first I thought there was but one. One appeared to answer the other—and sometimes they both sung together. Even as if the old were teaching her young. It was not the usual spring note of this bird—but a simple, clean, *pe-e-e-eet* rising steadily with one impulse to the end. They were undistinguishable in tone and rhythm—though one which I thought might be the younger was feebler. In the meanwhile as it was perched on the twig it was incessantly turning its head about looking for insects—and suddenly would dart aside or downward a rod or two and I could hear its bill snap as it caught one. Then it returned to the same or another perch.

August 19, 1853

The river is full and overflowing though there are still a few lilies and pontederias left. The wind comes from the northwest and is bracing and encouraging—and we can now sail up the stream. Flocks of bobolinks go tinkling along about the low willows—and swallows twitter—and a kingbird hovers almost stationary in the air a foot above the water.... Start up three blue herons in the meadow under Fair Haven—which fly heavily like bitterns with their breastbones projecting like a broad keel—or was it their necks curled up?

Mowing in Conant's meadow by Fair Haven. These mowers must often find the bittern's eggs. On entering Fair Haven with a fair wind scare up two ducks behind the point of the island. Saw three or four more in the afternoon. Also I hear from over the pond the clear metallic scream of young hawks—so common at this season—probably marsh hawks. . . .

We landed at the first cedar hills above the causeway—and ate our dinner and watermelon on them. A great reddish brown marsh hawk circling over the meadow there. . . .

Entered Fair Haven at sunset. A large hawk sat on the very top of a tall white pine in Lee's wood looking down at us. He looked like an eagle with his full breast—or like a great cone belonging to the tree. It is their habit thus to perch on the top of the pines and they are not readily detected. I could see him nearly half a mile off.

Immature great blue heron

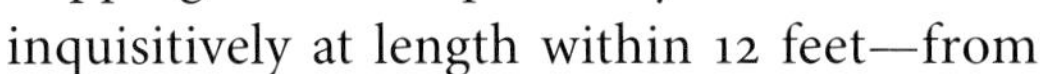
Yellow-billed cuckoo

August 20, 1857

As I stand there I hear a pecu liar sound which I mistake for a woodpecker's tapping—but I soon see a [yellow-billed] cuckoo hopping near suspiciously or inquisitively at length within 12 feet—from time to time uttering a hard dry note, very much like a woodpecker tapping a dead dry tree rapidly—its *full* clear white throat and breast toward me, and slowly lifting its tail from time to time. Though somewhat allied to that throttled note it makes by night, it was quite different from that.

August 21, 1859

In many holes in the meadow—made by the ice—the water having dried up I see many small fishes—pouts and pickerel and bream left dead and dying.... The blue heron must find it easy to get its living now. Are they not more common on our river such years as this?

In holes where the water has just evaporated leaving the mud moist I see a hundred little holes near together—with occasionally an indistinct track of a bird between. Measuring these holes I find them to be some two inches deep—or about the length of a snipe's bill and doubtless they were made by them. I start one snipe.

August 22, 1853

A peetweet *flew* along the shore and uttered its peculiar note. Their wings appear double as they fly by you—while their bill is cumbrously carried pointing downward in front.

August 23, 1858

I see a golden-crowned thrush—but it is silent except a chip. Sitting low on a twig near the main stem of a tree in these deep woods....

The *chewink* note of a chewink (not common) also a cuckoo's note.

August 24, 1852

The year is but a succession of days and I see that I could assign some office to each day—which summed up would be the history of the year. Everything is done in season and there is no time to spare. The bird gets its brood hatched in season and is off. I looked into the nest where I saw a vireo feeding its young a few days ago—but it is empty—it is fledged and flown.

August 25, 1860

See a large hen hawk sailing over Hubbard's meadow and Clamshell—soaring at last very high—and toward the north. At last it returns southward at that height impelling itself steadily and swiftly forward with its wings set in this wise: i.e. more curved or as it were trailing behind—without apparent motion. It thus moves half a mile directly. . . .

As I row by—see a green bittern nearby standing erect on Monroe's boat. Finding that it is observed—it draws in its head and stoops to conceal itself. When it flies it *seems* to have no tail. It allowed me to approach so near—apparently being deceived by some tame ducks there.

Green heron

Bobolink

August 26, 1859

The first fall rain is a memorable occasion—when the river is raised and cooled—and the first crop of sere and yellow leaves falls. The air is cleared—the dog days are over—sun sparkles are seen on water—crickets sound more distinct—saw grass reveals its spikes in the shorn fields—sparrows and bobolinks fly in flocks more and more.

August 27, 1852

Lower leaves of the smooth sumac are red. Hear *chic-a-day-day-day*—and crows. But for music reduced almost to the winter quire. Young partridges two thirds grown burst away. Globular galls on young oaks green on one side red on the other.

August 28, 1859

P.M.—To Walden.

A cool day, wind northwest—need a half-thick coat. Thus gradually we withdraw into winter quarters. It is a clear flashing air—and the shorn fields now look bright and yellowish and cool. Tinkled and twittered over by bobolinks—goldfinches—sparrows—etc. You feel the less inclined to bathing this weather—and bathe from principle, when boys, who bathe for fun, omit it.

August 29, 1858

Purple martin

Returning rather late P.M.—we saw some 40 martins sitting in a row and twittering on the ridge of his [Jacob Farmer's] *old* house—apparently preparing to migrate. He had never seen it before. Soon they all took to flight and filled the air in the neighborhood.

August 30, 1854

Hear a warbling vireo faintly on the elms. . . .

Was not that a meadow hen which I scared up in two places by the riverside—of a dark brown like a small woodcock—though it flew *straight* and low? . . .

Are they not young hen hawks which I have seen sailing for a week past—without red tails? . . .

I see brown thrashers on the black cherry tree—and hear their sharp clicks like a squirrel.

August 31, 1852

It is a bright and breezy day. I hear the note of goldfinches. . . . I see crows feeding on the meadow—large and black. . . .

I see and hear the kingfisher with his disproportionate black head or crest. The pigeon woodpecker darts across the valley—a catbird mews in the alders—a great bittern flies sluggishly away from his pine tree perch on Tupelo Cliff—digging his way through the air. These and crows—at long intervals are all the birds seen or heard. . . .

I saw a small hawk fly along under the hillside and alight on the ground, its breast and belly pure downy white. It was a very handsome bird. Though they are not fitted to walk much on the ground—but to soar—yet its feet which are but claws to seize its prey and hold to its perch are handsome appendages—and it is a very interesting sight on the ground. Yet there is a certain unfitness in so fair a breast—so pure white—made to breast nothing less pure than the sky or clouds—coming so nearly in contact with the earth. Never bespattered with the mud of earth. That was the impression made on me—of a very pure breast accustomed to float on the sky, in contact with the earth. It stood quite still watching me as if it was not easy for it to walk. I forgot to say that I saw nighthawks sailing about in the middle of the day. . . .

A flock of half a dozen or more blue-winged teal scared up downstream behind me as I was rowing have circled round to reconnoiter and cross upstream before me—quite close. I had seen another flock of ducks high in the air in the course of the day. Have ducks then begun—to return.

Blue-winged teal

SEPTEMBER

September 1, 1860

See how artfully the seed of a cherry is placed in order that a bird may be compelled to transport it. It is placed in the very midst of a tempting pericarp so that the creature that would devour a cherry must take a stone into its mouth. The bird is bribed with the pericarp to take the stone with it and do this little service for nature. Cherries are especially birds' food—and many kinds are called birds' cherry—and unless we plant the seeds occasionally, I shall think the birds have the best right to them.

Thus a bird's wing is added to the cherry stone—which was wingless—and it does not wait for winds to transport it.

September 2, 1851

What affinity is it brings the goldfinch to the sunflower—both yellow—to pick its seeds? . . .

Raise some sunflowers to attract the goldfinches, to feed them as well as your hens. What a broad and loaded, bounteously filled platter of food is presented this *bon-vivant*!

September 3, 1854

I see two or three large plump sparrows hopping along on the buttonbushes and eating the mikania blossoms, sometimes perching on the lower mossy stems and uttering a faint chip, with crown distinctly divided by a light line and another light line over eye, light throat and vent, ashy (?) breast and beneath, without spot. Is it not the white-throated sparrow?

White-throated sparrow

September 4, 1854

Now I began to hear owls—screech (?) owls at a distance upstream—but we hardly got nearer to them as if they retreated before us. At length when off Wheeler's grape and cranberry meadow we heard one near at hand. The rhythm of it was *pe-pe-ou*—this once or twice repeated but more of a squeal—and somewhat human. Or do not all strange sounds thrill us as *human*—till we have learned to refer them to their proper source. They appeared to answer one another half a mile apart—could be heard from far woods a mile off.

American golden plovers

September 5, 1854

Were those plump birds which looked somewhat like robins crossing the river yesterday P.M.—golden plover? I heard the upland plover note at same time, but these were much stouter birds. . . .

Saw a hummingbird about a cardinal flower—over the water's edge. . . . I see, as often before, a dozen doves on the rock—apparently for coolness—which fly before me.

September 6, 1854

The sun is rising directly over the eastern—magnetic east—end of the street. Not yet the equinox. I hear a faint warbling vireo on the elms still—in the morning.

September 7, 1857

Returning to my boat at the white maple I see a small round flock of birds—perhaps [red-winged] blackbirds—dart through the air, as thick as a charge of shot—now comparatively thin with regular intervals of sky between them—like the holes in the strainer of a watering pot—now dense and dark—*as if* closing up their ranks when they roll over one another and stoop downward.

September 8, 1851

Do not the song of birds and the fireflies go with the grass? While the grass is fresh the earth is in its vigor. The greenness of the grass is the best symptom or evidence of the earth's youth or health. Perhaps it will be found that when the grass ceases to be fresh and green or after June—the birds have ceased to sing—and that the fireflies too no longer in *myriads* sparkle in the meadows.

September 9, 1858

Watched a little dipper [pied-billed grebe] some ten rods off with my glass—but I could see no white on the breast. It was all black and brownish—and head not enlarged. Who knows how many little dippers are sailing and sedulously diving now along the edge of the pickerel-weed and the buttonbushes on our river! Unsuspected by most. This hot September P.M. all may be quiet amid the weeds—but the dipper and the bittern and the yellow-legs—and the blue heron and the rail—are silently feeding there. At length the walker who sits meditating on a distant bank sees the little dipper sail out from amid the weeds—and busily dive for its food along their edge. Yet ordinary eyes might range up and down the river all day—and never detect its small black head above the water.

Pied-billed grebe

September 10, 1854

As for birds:

About *ten* days ago *especially* I saw many large hawks—probably hen hawks and young, about.

Within a week several of the small slate-colored—and black-tipped hawks.

August 20th saw a sucker which I suppose must have been caught by a fish hawk.

Hear screech owls and hooting owls these evenings.

Have not noticed blue jays of late. *Occasionally* hear the *phebe* note of chickadees.

Partridges probably cease to mew for their young. For about three weeks have seen one or two small dippers. For ten days a *few* wood—and probably black ducks.

Small flocks of bluebirds about apple trees.

Larks common—but have not heard them sing for some time.

September 11, 1851

I started a great bittern from the weeds at the swimming place.

September 12, 1858

Amid the October woods we hear no funeral bell—but the scream of the jay.

September 13, 1858

Muskmelons and squashes are turning yellow in the gardens and ferns in the swamps.

Hear many warbling vireos these mornings. Many yellow butterflies in road and fields—all the country over.

September 14, 1854

6 A.M. to Hill. I hear a vireo still in the elms. The banks have now *begun* fairly to be sugared with the *A. Tradescanti* [small white aster]. I get very near a small dipper behind Dodd's—which sails out from the weeds fairly before me—then scoots over the surface crosswise the river throwing the water high—dives and is lost....

Blue jay

We see half a dozen herons in this voyage. Their wings are so long in proportion to their bodies—that there seems to be more than one undulation to a wing as they are disappearing in the distance and so you can distinguish them. You see another begin before the first has ended. It is remarkable how common these birds are about our sluggish and marshy river—we must attract them from a wide section of country. It abounds in those fenny districts—and meadow pond holes in which they delight. A flock of 13 telltales, great yellow-legs—start up with their shrill whistle from the midst of the great Sudbury meadow—and away they *sail in a flock* (a *sailing* or skimming *flock* that is something rare methinks) showing their white tails to alight in a more distant place. We see some small dippers and scare up many ducks—black mostly—which probably came as soon as the earliest. The great bittern too rises from time to time slowly flapping his way along at no great height above the meadow.

September 15, 1858

I have not seen nor heard a bobolink for some days at least—numerous as they were three weeks ago and even 15 days. They depart early. I hear a [white-breasted] nuthatch occasionally—but it reminds me of winter....

A hummingbird in the garden.

September 16, 1852

What makes this such a day for hawks? There are eight or ten in sight from the Cliffs large and small—one or more with a white rump. I detected the transit of the first by his shadow on the rock—and I look toward the sun for him. Though he is made light beneath to conceal him—his shadow betrays him. A hawk must get out of the wood—must get above it where he can sail. It is narrow dodging for him amid the boughs. He cannot be a hawk there, but only perch gloomily. Now I see a large one—perchance an eagle I say to myself!—down in the valley—circling and circling. Higher and wider—this way he comes—how beautiful does he repose on the air in the moment when he is directly over you—and you see the form and texture of his wings.

September 17, 1860

See a flock of 8 or 10 wood ducks on the Grindstone Meadow—with glass some 25 rods off—several drakes very handsome. They utter a *creaking scream* as they sail there being alarmed—from time to time—shrill and loud, very unlike the black duck. At last one sails off calling the others by a short creaking note.

September 18, 1858

I noticed that the wing of the peetweet—which is about two inches wide—has a conspicuous and straight-edged white bar along its middle on the underside. For half its length is 7/8 of an inch wide—and being quite parallel with the darker parts of the wing—it produces that singular effect in its flying which I have noticed. This line by the way is not mentioned by Wilson—yet it is perhaps the most noticeable mark of the bird when flying! The underside of the wings is commonly slighted in the description—though it is at least as often seen by us as the upper.

Spotted sandpiper in flight

Wood duck (male)

September 19, 1858

Hear a chewink's *chewink*. But how ineffectual is the note of a bird now! We hear it as if we heard it not—and forget it immediately. In spring it makes its due impression—and for a long time will not have done *echoing*, as it were, through our minds. It is even as if the atmosphere were in an unfavorable condition for this kind of music. Every musician knows how much depends on this.

September 20, 1851

I scare up the great bittern in meadow by the Heywood Brook near the ivy. He rises buoyantly as he flies against the wind and sweeps south over the willow with outstretched neck surveying. . . .

I see ducks or teal flying silent swift and straight the wild creatures.

September 21, 1852

The small skullcap and cress and the mullein still in bloom. I see pigeon woodpeckers oftener now with their light rears. . . .

My friend is he who can make a good guess at me—hit me on the wing.

Sharp-shinned hawk

September 22, 1852

Some of those I see are probably the sharp-shinned hawk. When was it I heard the upland plover? Has been a great flight of blue-winged teal this season.

September 23, 1860

I hear that a large owl, *probably* a cat owl, killed and carried off a full-grown turkey in Carlisle a few days ago.

September 24, 1854

I see still what I take to be small flocks of grackles—feeding beneath the covert of the buttonbushes—and flitting from bush to bush. They seldom expose themselves long.

September 25, 1851

In these cooler—windier—crystal days the note of the jay sounds a little more native. Standing on the Cliffs I see them flitting and screaming from pine to pine beneath—displaying their gaudy blue pinions. Hawks too I perceive sailing about in the clear air—looking white against the green pines—like the seeds of the milkweed. There is almost always a pair of hawks. Their shrill scream—that of the owls and wolves are all related.

September 26, 1857

I watch a marsh hawk circling low along the edge of the meadow looking for a frog—and now at last it alights to rest on a tussock.

September 27, 1852

It must have been a turtle dove [mourning dove] that eyed me so near—turned its head sideways to me for a fair view—looking with a St. Vitus twitching of its neck as if to recover its balance on an unstable perch—that is their way.

Mourning doves

September 28, 1851

A considerable part of the last two nights and yesterday—a steady and rather warm rain such as we have not had for a long time. This morning it is still completely overcast and drizzling a little. Flocks of small birds—apparently sparrows, bobolinks, or some bird of equal size with a penciled breast which makes a musical clucking—and piping goldfinches are flitting about like leaves and hopping up on to the bent grass stems in the garden, letting themselves down to the heavy heads, either shaking or picking out a seed or two, then alight to pick it up. I am amused to see them hop up on to the slender drooping grass stems then slide down or let themselves down as it were foot over foot—with great fluttering, till they can pick at the head and release a few seeds then alight to pick them up. They seem to prefer a coarse grass which grows like a weed in the garden between the potato hills—also the amaranth.

American goldfinch

September 29, 1858

See what must be a solitary tattler [solitary sandpiper] feeding by water's edge—and it has tracked the mud all about. It cannot be the *Tringa pectoralis* [*Calidris melanotos*, pectoral sandpiper]—for it has no conspicuous white chin nor black dashes on the throat—nor brown on the back and wings—and I think I see the round white spots on its wings. It has not the white on wing of the peetweet—yet utters the *peetweet* note! *short* and faint not protracted—and not the "sharp whistle" that Wilson speaks of.

September 30, 1857

At Wheeler's Wood by railroad heard a cat owl hooting at 3:30 P.M.—which was repeatedly answered by another some 40 rods off.

Talked with Minott who was sitting as normal in his woodshed. . . . I was telling him how some crows two or three weeks ago came flying with a scolding caw toward me as I stood on Cornel Rock and alighted within 50 feet on a dead tree above my head—unusually bold. Then away go all but one perchance to a tall pine in the swamp 20 rods off—anon he follows. Again they go quite out of sight amid the treetops—leaving one behind. This one at last quite at his leisure flaps away cawing—knowing well where to find his mates—though you might think he must winter alone.

Minott said that as he was going over to Lincoln one day 30 or 40 years ago—taking his way through Ebby Hubbard's woods—he heard a great flock of crows cawing over his head, and one alighted just within gunshot. He raised his little gun marked London—which he knew would fetch down anything that was within gunshot—and down came the

Solitary sandpiper

crow—but he was not killed, only so filled with shot that he could not fly. As he was going by John Wyman's at the pond—with the live crow in his hand—Wyman asked him what he was going to do with that crow. To which he answered nothing in particular, he happened to alight within gunshot—and so he shot him. Wyman said that he'd like to have him. What do you want to do with him asked M. If you'll give him to me I'll tell you—said the other. To which Minott said you may have him and welcome. Wyman then proceeded to inform him that the crows had eaten a great space in Josh Jones the blacksmith's cornfield which Minott had passed just below the almshouse—and that Jones had told him that if he could kill a crow in his cornfield he would give him half a bushel of rye. He could guess what he wanted the crow for. So Wyman took the crow and the next time he went into town he tossed him over the wall into the cornfield and then shot him—and carrying the dead crow to Jones, he got his half bushel of rye.

OCTOBER

October 1, 1858

Minott tells of a great rise of the river once in August—when a great many "marsh birds" as peeps—killdees [killdeers]—yellow-legs etc.—came inland—and he saw a flock of them reaching from Flint's Bridge a mile downstream over the meadows—and making a great noise.

Killdeer

October 2, 1859

As I sat on an old pigeon stand, not used this year on the hill south of the swamp—at the foot of a tree set up with perches nailed on it—a pigeon hawk [merlin], as I take it, came and perched on the tree. As if it had been wont to catch pigeons at such places.

October 3, 1852

Hear the loud laughing of a loon on Flint's—apparently alone in the middle. A wild sound heard far and suited to the wildest lake. Many acorns strew the ground and have fallen into the water.

Merlin

Common loon

October 4, 1859

Going over the large hillside stubble field west of Holden Wood—I start up a large flock of shore larks—hear their *sreet sreet* and *sreet sreet sreet*—and see their tails dark beneath. They are very wary—and run in the stubble for the most part invisible while one or two appear to act the sentinel on rock, peeping out behind it perhaps, and give their note of alarm—when away goes the whole flock. Such a flock circled back and forth several times over my head, just like ducks reconnoitering before they alight. If you look with a glass you are surprised to see how alert these spies are. When they alight in some stubbly hollow they set a watch or two on the rocks—to look out for foes. They have dusky bills and legs.

October 5, 1860

We came out on the east shore of Walden. The water is tolerably smooth. The smooth parts are dark and dimpled by many rising fish. Where it is rippled it is light colored—and the surface thus presents three or four alternate light and dark bars. I see a fish hawk skimming low over it—suddenly dive or stoop for one of these little fishes that rise to the surface so abundantly at this season. He then sits on a bare limb over the water, ready to swoop down again on his finny prey—presenting as he sits erect a long white breast and belly—and a white head.

No doubt he well knows the habits of these little fishes which dimple the surface of Walden at this season—and I doubt if there is any better fishing ground for him to resort to. He can easily find a perch overlooking the lake and discern his prey in the clear water.

Osprey

October 6, 1856

The reflections of the bright tinted maples very perfect. The common notes of the chickadee—so rarely heard for a long time—and also one *phebe* strain from it amid the leaning hemlocks—reminds me of pleasant winter days when they are more commonly seen. The jay's shrill note is more *distinct* of late about the edges of the woods—when so many birds have left us.

October 7, 1860

Rice says that when a boy, playing with darts with his brother Israel, one of them sent up his dart where a flock of crows was going over. One of the crows followed it down to the earth—picked it up, and flew off with it a quarter of a mile before it dropped it.

October 8, 1860

Standing by a [passenger] pigeon place on the north edge Damon's lot—I saw on the dead top of a white pine four or five rods off (which had been stripped for 15 feet downward that it might die and afford with its branches a perch for the pigeons about the place—like the more artificial ones that were set up) two woodpeckers that were new to me. They uttered a peculiar sharp *kek kek* on alighting (not so sharp as that of the hairy or downy woodpecker) and appeared to be about the size of the hairy woodpecker, or between that and the golden-winged. I had a good view of them with my glass as long as I desired. With their back to me, they were clean black all above—as well as their feet and bills—and each had a yellow or orange (or possibly orange scarlet?) front (the anterior part of the head at the base of the upper mandible).

A long white line along the side of the head to the neck—with a black one below it. The breast, as near as I could see, was gray

Black-backed woodpecker

specked with white—and the underside of the wing expanded was also gray—with small white spots. The throat white and vent also white or whitish. Is this the arctic three-toed [black-backed woodpecker]? (Not of Nuttall.) Probably many trees dying on this large burnt tract will attract many woodpeckers to it.

October 9, 1857

Saw a jay stealing corn from a stack in a field.

October 10, 1851

As I stood amid the witch hazels—near Flint's Pond—a flock of a dozen chickadees came flitting and sing about me with great ado—a most cheering and enlivening sound. With incessant *day-day-day*—and a fine wiry strain betweenwhiles—flitting ever nearer and nearer and nearer, inquisitively—till the boldest was within five feet of me—then suddenly, their curiosity satiated they flit by degrees further away and disappear. And I hear with regret their retreating *day-day-days*.

October 11, 1856

The sproutland and stubble behind the cliffs are all alive with restless flocks of sparrows of various species.... They are continually flitting past and surging upward, two or more in pursuit of each other, in the air—where they break like waves—and pass along with a faint *cheep*. On the

Chipping sparrow

least alarm many will rise from a juniper bush—on to a shrub oak above it—and, when all is quiet return into the juniper—perhaps for its berries. It is often hard to detect them as they sit on the young trees now beginning to be bare for they are very nearly the color of the bark—and are very cunning to hide behind the leaves. There are apparently two other kinds one like purple finches another more like large Savannah sparrows.

October 12, 1852

Paddled on Walden. A rippled surface—scared up ducks. Saw them first far over the surface just risen—two smaller white-bellied, one larger black. They circled round as usual and the first went off—but the black one went round and round and over the pond five or six times at a considerable height and distance when I thought several times he had gone to the river and at length settled down by a slanting flight of a quarter of a mile into a distant part of the pond which I had left free—but what beside safety these ducks get by sailing in the middle of Walden I don't know. That black rolling pin with wings circling round you half a mile off for a quarter of an hour—at that height, from which he sees the river and Fair Haven all the while—from which he sees so many things while I see almost him alone. Their wings set so far back. They are not handsome but wild.

October 13, 1852

It is a sufficiently clear and warm rather Indian summer day—and they are gathering the apples in the orchard. The warmth is more required and we welcome and appreciate it all. The shrub oak plain is now a deep red—with grayish withered apparently white oak leaves intermixed. The chickadees take heart too and sing above these warm rocks.

October 14, 1859

I see and hear of many hawks for some weeks past. On the 11th I saw one as small as I ever saw—I thought not larger than a kingbird, as I stood on the Cliffs—hovering over the wood about on a level with me. It sailed directly only a rod or two—then flapped its wings fast and sailed on a rod or two further. Was it not a sparrow hawk [American kestrel]?

American kestrel

Hairy woodpecker

October 15, 1852

The flight of a partridge—leaving her lair (?) on the hillside only a few rods distant with a gentle whirring sound—is like the blowing of rocks at a great distance. Perhaps it produces the same kind of undulations in the air.

October 16, 1859

See a hairy woodpecker on a burnt pitch pine. He distinctly rests on his tail constantly. With what vigor he taps and bores the bark making it fly far and wide. And then darts off with a sharp whistle.

October 17, 1855

I saw behind (or rather *in front of*) me as I rowed home a little dipper appear in midriver as if I had passed right over him. It dived while I looked—and I could not see it come up anywhere.

October 18, 1855

There are a great many crows scattered about on the meadow. What do they get to eat there. Also I scare up a dozen larks at once. A large brown marsh hawk comes beating the bush along the river—and ere

Adult male northern harrier

long a slate-colored one (male)—with black tips is seen circling against a distant woodside. I scare up in midst of the meadows a great many dark colored sparrows—one or two at a time—which go off with a note somewhat like the lesser redpoll's. Some migrating kind, I think. . . .

There is no life perceptible on this broad meadow except what I have named. The crows are very conspicuous—black against the green.

October 19, 1856

See quite a flock of myrtle birds—which I might carelessly have mistaken for slate-colored snowbirds—flitting about on the rocky hillside under Conantum Cliff. They show about three white or light colored spots when they fly—*commonly* no bright yellow—though some are pretty bright. They perch on the side of the dead mulleins—on rocks—on the ground—and directly dart off apparently in pursuit of some insect. I hear no note from them. They are thus near or on the ground there not as in spring.

October 20, 1857

I had gone but little way on the old Carlisle road when I saw Brooks Clark who is now about 80 and bent like a bow hastening along the road bare-footed as usual—with an axe in his hand. Was in haste perhaps on account of the cold wind on his bare feet. . . . When he got up to me I saw that besides the axe in one hand, he had his shoes in the other filled with knurly apples and a dead robin. . . . I asked if he had found the robin dead. No, he said, he found it with its wing broken and killed it—he also added, that he had found some apples in the woods, and as he hadn't anything to carry them in he put 'em in his shoes. . . .

It pleased me to see this cheery old man—with such a feeble hold on life—bent almost double, thus enjoying the evening of his days. . . . Better his robin than your turkey—his shoes full of apples than your barrels full. They will be sweeter and suggest a better tale. He can afford to tell how he *got* them and we to listen. There is an old wife too at home to share them and hear how they were obtained—like an old squirrel shuffling to his hole with a nut.

October 21, 1857

I see many myrtle birds now about the house—this forenoon—on the advent of cooler weather. They keep flying up against the house and the window and fluttering there as if they would come in—or alight on the wood pile or pump. They would commonly be mistaken for sparrows—but show more white when they fly—beside the yellow on the rump and sides of breast seen near to and two white bars on the wings. Chubby birds. . . .

I see a robin eating prinos berries [winterberries]. Is not the robin the principal berry eating bird nowadays. There must be more about the barberry bushes in Melvin's Preserve than anywhere.

October 22, 1857

I see what I call a hermit thrush on the bushes by the shore of Flint's Pond—pretty tame. It has an olive brown back with a more ferruginous tail which [is] *very narrowly* tipped with whitish—an apparently cream-colored throat and dusky cream color beneath. The breast is richly spotted with black. The legs are flesh-colored and transparent—the bill black. Yet Wilson says the legs are dusky.

Hermit thrush

October 23, 1852

The red squirrel chirrups in the walnut grove. The chickadees flit along following me inquisitively a few rods with lisping tinkling note—flit within a few feet of me from curiosity—head downward on the pines.

Canada geese in flight

October 24, 1858

A northeast storm—though not much rain fallen today—but a fine driving mizzle or "drisk." This as usual brings the geese and at 2:30 P.M. I see two flocks go over—I hear that some were seen two or three weeks ago??—faintly honking. A great many must go over today—and also alight in this neighborhood. This weather warns them of the approach of winter—and this wind speeds them on their way. Surely, then, while geese fly overhead—we can live here as contentedly as they do at York Factory on Hudson's Bay. We shall perchance be as well provisioned and have as good society as they. Let us be of good cheer, then, and expect an annual vessel which brings the spring to us, without fail.

October 25, 1853

Saw a telltale on Cheney's shore close to the water's edge. . . . It was all white below and dark above—with a pure white tail prettily displayed in flying. It kept raising its head with a jerk as if it had the St. Vitus' dance. It would alight in the water and swim like a little duck. Once, when I went ashore and started it—it flew so as to bring a willow between it and me

Greater yellowlegs

and alighted quite near much nearer than before to spy me. When it went off it uttered a sharp *te-te-te-te-te* flying with quivering wings—dashing about. I think that the storm of yesterday and last night brought it up.

October 26, 1857

At the hewing place on the flat above many sparrows are flitting past amid the birches and sallows. They are chiefly *F. hyemalis*. How often they may be thus flitting along in a straggling manner—from bush to bush—so that the hedgerow will be all alive with them—each uttering a faint chip from time to time as if to keep together—bewildering you so that you know not if the greater part are gone by or still to come.

One rests but a moment on the tree before you and is gone again. You wonder if they know whither they are bound and how their leader is appointed.

October 27, 1860

As I am coming out of this [white pine wood] looking for seedling oaks I see a jay, which was screaming at me, fly to a white oak eight or ten rods from the wood in the pasture—and directly alight on the ground—pick up an acorn and fly back into the woods with it. This was one—perhaps the most effectual way in which this wood was stocked with the numerous little oaks which I saw—under that dense white pine grove.

Where will you look for a jay sooner than in a dense pine thicket. It is there they commonly live, and build. . . .

What if the oaks are far off? Think how quickly a jay can come and go, and how many times in a day!

Blue jay

October 28, 1857

I look up and see a male marsh hawk with his clean cut wings that has just skimmed past above my head—not at all disturbed—only tilting his body a little now 20 rods off with demi-semi-quaver of his wings. He is a very neat flyer.

Again I hear the scream of a hen hawk soaring and circling onward. I do not often see the marsh hawk *thus*.

What a regular figure this fellow makes on high with his broad tail and broad wings! Does he perceive me that he rises higher and circles to one side. He goes round now one full circle without a flap tilting his wing a little. Then *flaps* three or four times and *rises* higher. Now he comes on like a billow—screaming. Steady as a planet in its orbit—with his head bent down—but on second thought that small sproutland seems worthy of a longer scrutiny and he gives one circle backward over it. His scream is somewhat like the whinnering of a horse—if it is not rather a *split squeal*. It is a hoarse tremulous breathing forth of his winged energy. But why is it so regularly repeated at that height? Is it to scare his prey that he may see by its motion where it is—or to inform its mate or companion of its whereabouts? Now he crosses the at present broad river steadily—deserving to have one or two rabbits at least to swing about him. What majesty there is in this small bird's flight! The hawks are large-souled.

October 29, 1860

Again, as day before yesterday, sitting on the edge of a pine wood I see a jay fly to a white oak half a dozen rods off in the pasture and gathering an acorn from the ground—hammer away at it under its foot on a limb of the oak—with an awkward and rapid seesaw or teetering motion it had to lift its head so high to acquire the requisite momentum. The jays scold about almost every white oak tree—since we hinder their coming to it.

October 30, 1853

I see tree sparrows in loose flocks chasing one another on the alders and willows by the brookside. They keep up a general low and incessant twittering warble as if suppressed—very sweet at this season—but not heard far. It is as Wilson says, *like* a chip-bird—but this has a spot commonly on breast

American tree sparrow

and a bright chestnut crown. It is quite striped (bay and brown with dark) above and has a forked tail. I am not quite sure that I have seen them before.

They are a chubby bird—and have not the stripes on the breasts which the song sparrow has. The last moreover has not that striped bay and blackish and ash above. By the bathing place I see a song sparrow—with his full striped breast. He drops stealthily behind the wall and skulks amid the bushes—now sits behind a post, and peeps round at me—ever restless and quirking his tail—and now and then uttering a faint *chip*. It is not so light beneath as the last.

October 31, 1858

Get a good sight on Conantum of a sparrow (such as I have seen in flocks some time) which utters a sharp *te-te-te* quickly repeated—as it flies—sitting on a wall three or four rods off. I see that it is rather long and slender—is perhaps dusky ash above with some black backward—has a pretty long black bill—a white ring about eye—white chin—and line under cheek—a black (or dark) spotted breast—and dirty cream color beneath—legs long and slender and perhaps reddish brown—two faint light bars on wings. But what distinguishes it more—it keeps gently jerking or tossing its tail as it sits—and when a flock flies over you see the tails distinctly black beneath. Though I detected no yellow yet I think from the note that it must be the shore lark (such as I saw March 24th) in their fall plumage. They are a common bird at this season, I think.

Horned lark

NOVEMBER

November 1, 1851

It is a rare qualification to be able to state a fact simply and adequately. To digest some experience cleanly. To say yes and no with authority. To make a square edge. To conceive and suffer the truth to pass through us living and intact—even as a waterfowl an eel—thus peopling new waters. . . .

It is a bright clear warm November day. I feel blessed. I love my life. I warm toward all nature.

The woods are now much more open than when I last observed them—the leaves have fallen and they let in light and I see the sky through them as through a crow's wing in every direction. . . .

Counted 125 crows in one straggling flock moving westward.

November 2, 1852

The prinos berries also now attract me in the scarcity of leaves—its own all gone—its berries are apparently a brighter red for it. The month of chickadees and new-swollen buds. At long intervals I see or hear a robin still. . . .

I do not know whether the perch amuse themselves thus more in the fall than at any other time. In such transparent and apparently bottomless water their swimming impresses the beholder as a kind of flight or hovering like a compact flock of birds passing below one—just beneath his level on the right or left.

November 3, 1852

At Andromeda Pond, started nine black (?) ducks just at sunset, as usual they circling far round to look at me.

November 4, 1851

It is truly a raw and gusty day and I hear a tree creak sharply like a bird—a phoebe. The hypericums [St. John's-wort] stand red or lake over the brook. The jays with their scream are at home in the scenery. . . . The slender chestnuts maples elms and white ash trees which last are uncommonly numerous here are now all bare of leaves—and a few small hemlocks with their now thin but unmixed and fresh green foliage stand over and cheer the stream and remind me of winter—the snows which are to come and drape them and contrast with their green—and the chickadees that are to flit and lisp amid them.

November 5, 1855

At Hubbard's Crossing I see a large male hen harrier [northern harrier] skimming over the meadow—its deep slate somewhat sprinkled or mixed with black—perhaps young. It flaps a little and then sails straight forward. So low it must rise at every fence. But I perceive that it follows the windings of the meadow over many fences.

Northern harrier

American pipit

November 6, 1853

It is remarkable how little we attend to what is passing before us constantly unless our genius directs our attention that way. There are these little sparrows with white tail [American pipit]—perhaps the prevailing bird of late—which have flitted before me so many falls and springs and yet they have been as it were strangers to me and I have not inquired whence they came or whither they were going, or what their habits were. It is surprising how little most of us are contented to know about the sparrows which drift about in the air before us just before the first snows.

November 7, 1853

The notes of one or two small birds this cold morning in the now comparatively leafless woods sound like a nail dropped on an anvil—or a glass pendant tinkling against its neighbor. . . .

Great straggling flocks of crows still flying westerly.

November 8, 1857

About 10 A.M. a long flock of geese are going over from northeast to southwest—or parallel with the general direction of the coast and great mountain ranges. The sonorous quavering sounds of the geese—are the voice of this cloudy air. A sound that comes from directly between us and the sky—an aerial sound—and yet so distinct heavy and sonorous. A clanking chain drawn through the heavy air.

Canada goose

Black-capped chickadee and cattail

November 9, 1850

The chickadees—if I stand long enough—hop nearer and nearer inquisitively from pine bough to pine bough till within four or five feet, occasionally lisping a note.

November 10, 1858

Hearing in the oak wood nearby a sound as if someone had broken a twig—I looked up and saw a jay pecking at an acorn. There were several jays busily gathering acorns on a scarlet oak. I could hear them break them off. They then flew to a suitable limb and placing the acorn under one foot, hammered away at it busily—looking round from time to time to see if any foe was approaching—and soon reached the meat—and nibbled at it, holding up their heads to swallow—while they held it very firmly with their claws. (Their hammering made a sound like the woodpeckers.) Nevertheless it sometimes dropped to the ground before they had done with it.

November 11, 1858

Going by the willow row above railroad scare up a small duck—*perhaps* teal—and in the withered grass at Nut Meadow Brook two black ducks—which rise black between me and the sun—but when they have circled round to the east show some silvery sheen on the underside of their wings. Am surprised to see a little ice in this brook in the shade, as I push far up it through a dense field of withered bluejoint—a spot white with frost—a few inches over. Saw a small pool in the woods also skimmed over—and many ice crystals heaved up in low ground. Scare up a bird which at first ran in the grass—then flew—a snipe. . . .

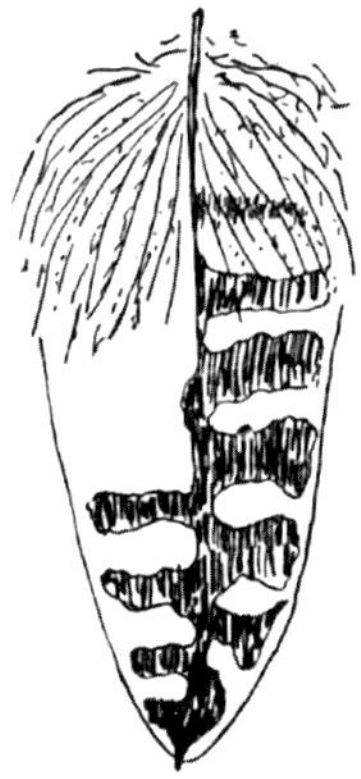

The tail coverts of the young hen hawk—i.e. this year's bird at present—are white very handsomely barred or watered with dark brown in an irregular manner somewhat as above—the bars on opposite sides of the midrib—alternating in an agreeable manner. Such natural objects have suggested the "watered" figures or colors in the arts. Few mortals ever look down on the tail coverts of a young hen hawk—yet these are not only beautiful, but of a peculiar beauty—being differently marked and colored (to judge from Wilson's account of the old) from those of the old bird. Thus she finishes her works above men's sight.

November 12, 1851

Minott has a story for every woodland path. He has hunted in them all. Where we walked last, he had once caught a partridge by the *wing*!

November 13, 1852

To Andromeda Ponds. Andromeda [bog rosemary] is a dull reddish brown like oak leaves. Saw a flock of little passenger birds by Walden—busily pecking at the white birch catkins—about the size of a chickadee—one *distinct* white bar on wings—most with dark penciled breast—some with whitish—forked tail—bright chestnut or crimson (?) frontlet [common redpoll]. . . . When startled they went off with a jingling sound somewhat like emptying a bag of coin.

November 14, 1855

Leaves and sticks and billets of wood come floating down in middle of the full still stream turning round in the eddies—and I mistake them for ducks at first. See two red-wing blackbirds alight on a black willow.

November 15, 1859

About the 23d of October I saw a large flock of goldfinches (judging from their motions and notes) on the tops of the hemlocks up the Assabet—apparently feeding on their seeds, then falling. They were collected in great numbers on the very tops of these trees and flitting from one to another. Rice has since described to me the same phenomenon as observed by him there since (says he saw the birds picking out the seeds) though he did not know what birds they were. William Rice says that these birds get so much of the lettuce seed that you can hardly save any. They get sunflower seeds also. Are called "lettuce birds" in the books.

November 16, 1850

I hear deep amid the birches some row among the birds or the squirrels where evidently some mystery is being developed to them. The jay is on the alert—mimicking every woodland note. What *has* happened? Who's dead? The twitter retreats before you and you are never let into the secret. Some tragedy surely is being enacted—but murder will out. How many little dramas are enacted in the depths of the woods at which man is not present!

November 17, 1859

I have been so absorbed of late in Captain Brown's fate—as to be surprised whenever I detected the old routine running still—met persons going about their affairs indifferent. It appeared strange to me that the *little dipper* should be still diving in the river as of yore. And this suggested that this grebe might be diving here when Concord shall be no more. Any affecting human event may blind our eyes to natural objects.

November 18, 1855

As I sat in the house I was struck with the brightness and heat of the sun reflected from this our first snow. There was an intenser light in the house and I felt an uncommon heat from the sun's rays on my back. The

Blue jay

air is very clear and the sky heavenly with a few floating downy clouds. I am prepared to hear sharp screaming notes rending the air, from the winter birds. I do in fact hear many jays—and the tinkling like rattling glass from chickadees and tree sparrows.

November 19, 1855

Speaking of geese—he [Minott] says that Dr. Hurd told a tough story once. He said that when he went out to the well there came a flock of geese flying so low that they had to rise to clear the well-sweep. M. says that there used to be a great many more geese formerly—he used to hear a great many flocks in a day go "yelling" over.

November 20, 1857

Some bank swallows' nests are exposed by the caving of the bank at Clamshell. The very smallest hole is about 2½ inches wide horizontally, and barely one high. All are much wider than high (vertically). One nest with an egg in it still is

Bank swallow colony in summer

completely exposed. The cavity at the end is shaped like a thick hoe cake or lens about six inches wide and two plus thick vertically. The nest is a regular but shallow one made simply of stubble—about five inches in diameter, and ¾ inches deep.

November 21, 1857

Just above the grape-hung birches my attention was drawn to a singular looking dry leaf or parcel of leaves on the shore about a rod off. Then I thought it might be the dry and yellowed skeleton of a bird with all its ribs—then the shell of a turtle—or possibly some large dry oak leaves peculiarly curved and cut. And then all at once I saw that it was a woodcock—perfectly still with its head drawn in standing on its great pink feet. I had, apparently, noticed only the yellowish brown portions of the plumage—referring the dark brown to the shore behind it. May it not be that the yellowish brown markings of the bird correspond somewhat to its skeleton? At any rate with my eye steady on it from a point within a rod, I did not for a considerable time suspect it to be a living creature. Examining the shore after it had flown with a whistling flight—I saw that there was a clear space of mud between the water and the edge of ice crystals about two inches wide—melted so far by the lapse of the water—and all along the edge of the ice for a rod or two at least there was a hole where it had thrust its bill down—probing every ½ inch, frequently closer. Some animal life must be collected at that depth just in that narrow space—savory morsels for this bird.

American woodcock

November 22, 1853

Geese went over yesterday and today also....

As I was returning down the river toward night—I mistook the creaking of a plow wheel for a flock of blackbirds passing overhead—but it is too late for them.

November 23, 1853

The cocks are the only birds I hear—but they are a host. They crow as freshly and bravely as ever—while poets go down the stream—degenerate into science and prose. I have not seen a flock of small birds—either tree sparrows—or *F. hyemalis*—or white in tails etc. for about a fortnight. There is now no sound of early birds on the leafless trees and bushes—willows and alders along this water course. The few that are left probably roost in the evergreen woods. Yet I hear—or seem to hear the faintest possible lisp or creak from some sparrow as if from a crack in the mist-clad earth or some ox yoke—or distant wain. I suspect that the song sparrow lingers as late here and there alone as any migrating bird. . . .

The Indian summer itself—said to be more remarkable in this country than elsewhere—no less than the reblossoming of certain flowers—the peep of the hylodes [tree frogs]—and sometimes the faint warble of some birds—is the reminiscence or rather the return of spring. The year renewing its youth.

At 5 P.M. I saw flying southwest high overhead a flock of geese—and heard the faint honking of one or two. They were in the usual harrow form—12 in the shorter line and 24 in the longer—the latter abutting on the former at the fourth bird from the front. I judged *hastily* that the interval between the geese was about double their alar extent and as the last is according to Wilson 5 9/12 feet, the former may safely be called eight feet. I hear they were fired at with a rifle from Bunker Hill the other day.

This is the sixth flock I have seen or heard of since the morning of the 17th, i.e. within a week.

November 24, 1851

Setting stakes in the swamp (Ministerial). Saw seven black ducks fly out of the peat hole. Saw there also a tortoise still stirring. The painted tortoise I believe.

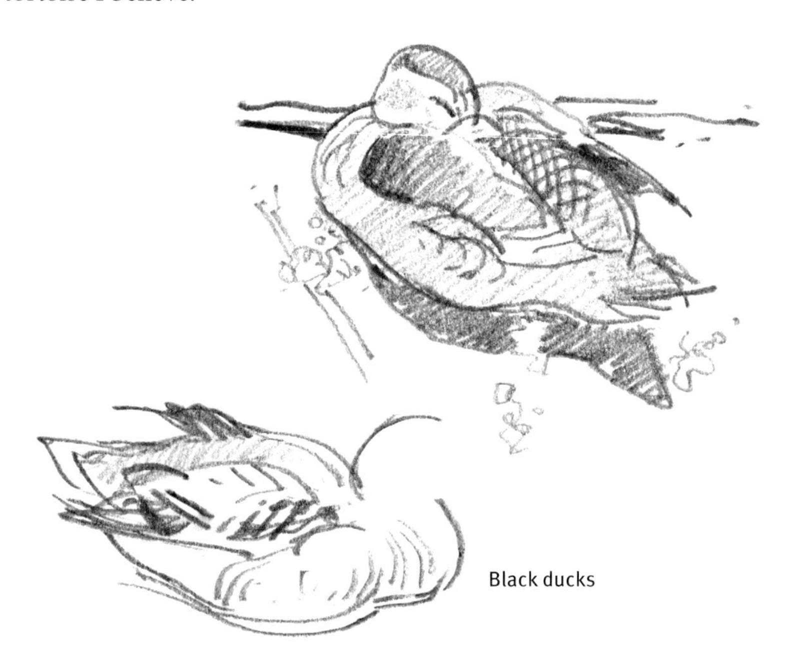

Black ducks

Crows in a plowed field

November 25, 1860

As I go up the meadowside toward Clamshell I see a very great collection of crows far and wide on the meadows—evidently gathered by this cold and blustering weather. Probably the moist meadows where they feed are frozen up against them. They flit before me in countless numbers—flying very low on account of the strong northwest wind that comes over the hill—and a cold gleam is reflected from the back and wings of each, as from a weather stained shingle. Some perch within three or four rods of me—and seem weary. I see where they have been pecking the apples by the meadowside. An immense cohort of cawing crows which sudden winter has driven near to the habitations of man. When I return after sunset I see them collecting and hovering over and settling in the dense pine woods west of E. Wood's—as if about to roost there.

Yesterday I saw one flying over the house, its wings so curved by the wind that I thought it a black hawk.

November 26, 1860

While I am walking in the oak wood—or counting the rings of a stump—I hear the faint note of a nuthatch like the creak of a limb—and detect on the trunk of an oak much nearer than I suspected—and its mate or companion not far off. This is a constant phenomenon of the late fall or early winter—for we do not hear them in summer that I remember. I heard one not long since in the street. . . .

I saw that nuthatch today pick out from a crevice in the bark of an oak trunk—where it was perpendicular—something white once or twice and pretty large. May it not have been the meat of an acorn? Yet commonly they are steadily hopping about the trunks in search of insect food. Possibly some of those acorn shells I see about the base of trees may have been dropped from the crevices in the bark above by birds—nuthatch or jay—as well as left by squirrels.

White-breasted nuthatch

November 27, 1855

A man in Brighton whom he [J. Farmer] fully believes told him that he built a bower—near a dead horse—and placed himself within to shoot crows. One crow took his station as sentinel on the top of the tree—and 30 or 40 alighted upon the horse. He fired and killed seven or eight. But the rest instead of minding him immediately flew to their sentinel and pecked him to pieces before his eyes. Also Mr. Joseph Clark told him that as he was going along the road he cast a stick over the wall and hit some crows in a field—whereupon they flew directly at their sentinel on an apple tree and beat and buffeted him away to the woods as far as he could see.

November 28, 1857

P.M.—Around Ebby Hubbard's woodlot. On the hillside above his swamp near the Ministerial land I found myself walking in one of those shelf-like hillside paths—made by Indians, hunters, cows, or whatnot—and it was beset with fresh snares for partridges this wise. Upright twigs are stuck in the ground across the path a foot or more in height and just close enough together to turn a partridge aside—leaving a space about four inches wide in the middle. And some twigs are stretched across above to prevent the birds hopping over. Then a sapling about an inch in diameter or less is bent over and the end caught under one of the twigs which has a notch or projection on one side—and a free running noose attached to the sapling hangs in the

opening and is kept spread by being hung on some very slight nicks in the two twigs. This seems to suppose the bird to be going one way only—but perhaps if it cannot escape one way it will turn and try to go back—and so spring the trap. I see one that was sprung—with nothing in it—another whose slip-noose was blown or fallen one side—and another with a partridge still warm in it. It was a male bird hanging dead by the neck just touching its toes to the ground. It had a collar or ruff about its neck of large and conspicuous black feathers with a green reflection. This black is peculiar to the male—the female's being brown. Its feet now clinched in its agony were the strangest looking—pale blue—with a fine fringe, of scales or the like—on each side of each toe. The small black feathers were centered with gray spots. The scapulars were darker brown dashed with large clear pale brown spots—the breast feathers light with light brown marks. The tail feathers had each a broad black bar—except the middle one which was more mixed or grayish there. The bands of the females are said to be more brown—as is their collar. There were a few droppings of the bird close by the snare—in two instances. Were they dropped after it was caught? Or did they determine the locality of the snare?

These birds appear to run most along the sides of wooded banks around swamps—at least these paths and snares occur there oftenest. I *often* scare them up from amid or near hemlocks in the woods.

The general color of the bird is that of the ground and dry leaves on it at present. The bird hanging in the snare was very inconspicuous. I had gone close by it once without noticing it. Its wings are short and stout—and look as if they were a little worn by striking the ground or bushes—or perhaps in drumming. I observed a bare bright red or scarlet spot over each eye.

November 29, 1858

I see a living shrike caught today in the barn of the Middlesex House.

November 30, 1858

The shrike was very violent for a long time beating itself against the bars of its cage—at Stacy's. Today it is quiet and has eaten raw meat. Its plain dark ash colored crown and back are separated by a very distinct line from the black wings. It has a powerful hawk-like beak but slender legs and claws—close to it looks more like a muscicapa [flycatcher] than anything.

DECEMBER

December 1, 1856

Slate-colored snowbirds flit before me in the path—feeding on the seeds on the snow—the countless little brown seeds that begin to be scattered over the snow—so much the more obvious to bird and beast. A hundred kinds of indigenous grain are harvested now—broadcast upon the surface of the snow. Thus at a critical season these seeds are shaken down on to a clean white napkin, unmixed with dirt and rubbish—and off this the little pensioners pick them. Their clean table is thus spread a few inches or feet above the ground. Will wonder become extinct in me? Shall I become insensitive as a fungus?

December 2, 1852

The river has risen since the last rain—a few feet—and partially floods the meadow. See still two ducks on the meadow. Hear the jay in distant copses.

December 3, 1853

Saw two tree sparrows on Monroe's larch by the waterside. Larger than chip birds—with more bay above and a distinct white bar on wings—not to mention bright chestnut crown and obscure spot on breast—all beneath pale ash. They were busily and very adroitly picking the seeds out of the larch cones. It would take man's clumsy fingers a good while to get at one, and then only by breaking off the scales—but they picked them out as rapidly as if they were insects on the outside of the cone, uttering from time to time a faint tinkling chip.

American tree sparrow

December 4, 1856

Saw and heard cheep faintly one little tree sparrow—the neat chestnut-crowned and winged and white-barred bird—perched on a large and solitary white birch. So clean and tough—made to withstand the winter. This color reminds me of the upper side of the shrub oak leaf. I love the few homely colors of nature at this season—her strong wholesome browns—her sober and primeval grays—her celestial blue—her vivacious green—her pure cold snowy white.

December 5, 1853

Many living leaves are very dark red now, the only effect of the frost on them—the checkerberry—andromeda—low cedar—and more or less lambkill etc. Saw and heard a downy woodpecker on an apple tree. Have not many winter birds, like this and the chickadee, a sharp note like tinkling glass or icicles. The chip of the tree sparrow also and the whistle of the shrike, is it not wintry in the same way? And the sonorous hooting owl. But not so the jay and *Fringilla linaria* [common redpoll]—and still less the crow. Now for the short days and early twilight—in which I hear the sound of woodchopping. The sun goes down behind a low cloud and the world is darkened. The partridge is budding on the apple tree—and bursts away from the pathside.

December 6, 1852

Saw a great slate-colored hawk sail away from the Cliffs.

December 7, 1858

To Boston.

At *Natural History Rooms*. . . .

The rail's egg (of Concord, which I have seen) is not the Virginia rail's which is smaller and nearly pure white—nor the clapper rail's which is larger.

Is it the sora rail's? (Of which there is no egg in this collection.)

My egg found in R.W.E.'s garden is not the white-throated sparrow's egg.

Dr. Bryant calls my seringo (i.e. the faint-noted bird) Savannah sparrow. He says Cooper's hawk is just like the sharp-shinned, only a little larger commonly. He could not tell them apart. Neither he nor Brewer can identify eggs always. Could match some gulls' eggs out of another basket full of a different species as well as out of the same basket.

Cooper's hawk

December 8, 1855

This P.M. I go to the woods down the railroad—seeking the society of some flock of little birds, or some squirrel—but in vain. I only hear the faint lisp of—probably—a tree sparrow. I go through empty halls—apparently unoccupied by bird or beast. Yet it is cheering to walk there while the sun is reflected from far through the aisles with a silvery light from the needles of the pine. The contrast of light or sunshine and shade, though the latter is now so thin—is food enough for me. . . . In a little busy flock of lisping birds—chickadees or lesser redpolls [common redpolls]—even in a nuthatch or downy woodpecker—there would have been a sweet society for me—but I did not find. Yet I had the sun penetrating into the deep hollows through the aisles of the wood—and the silvery sheen of its reflection from masses of white pine needles.

December 9, 1856

The pond is perfectly smooth and full of light. I hear only the strokes of a lingering woodchopper at a distance—and the melodious hooting of an owl, which is as common and marked a sound as the axe or the locomotive whistle—yet where does the ubiquitous hooter sit and who sees him? In whose woodlot is he to be found? Few eyes have rested on him hooting. Few on him silent on his perch even. Yet cut away the woods never so much year after year—though the chopper has not seen him and only a grove or two is left, still his aboriginal voice is heard indefinitely far and sweet—mingled oft in strange harmony with the newly invented din of trade—like a sentence of Allegri sounded in our streets. Hooting from invisible perch at his foes the woodchoppers who are invading his domains. As the earth only a few inches beneath the surface is undisturbed and what it was anciently—so are heard still some primeval sounds in the air. Some of my townsmen I never see and of a great proportion I do not hear the voices in a year—though they live within my horizon—but every week almost I hear the loud voice of the hooting owl—though I do not see the bird more than once in ten years.

December 10, 1854

Weather warmer, snow softened. Saw a large flock of snow buntings (quite white against woods, at any rate) though it is quite warm. Snow fleas in paths. First I have seen. Hear the small woodpecker's whistle—not much else—only crows and partridges else—and chickadees.

December 11, 1855

Standing there though in this *bare* November landscape—I am reminded of the incredible phenomenon—of small birds in winter. That ere long amid the cold and powdery snow—as it were a fruit of the season will come twittering a flock of delicate crimson-tinged birds (lesser redpolls) to sport and feed on the seeds and buds now just ripe for them on the sunny side of a wood—shaking down the powdery snow there in their cheerful social feeding—as if it were high midsummer—to them. These crimson aerial creatures have wings which would bear them quickly to the regions of summer, but here is all the summer they want. What a rich contrast—tropical colors—crimson breasts—on cold white snow.

Such etherealness such delicacy in their forms—such ripeness in their colors in this stern and barren season. It is as surprising as if you were to find a brilliant crimson flower—which flourished amid snows. They greet the chopper and the hunter in their furs. . . .

When some rare northern bird like the pine grosbeak is seen thus far south in the winter—he does not suggest poverty—but dazzles us with his beauty. There is in them a warmth akin to the warmth that melts the icicle. Think of these brilliant warm-colored and richly warbling birds—birds of paradise—dainty-footed—downy-clad—in the midst of a New England—a Canadian winter. The woods and fields now somewhat solitary being deserted by their more tender summer residents are now frequented by these rich but delicately tinted and hardy northern immigrants of the air. Here is no imperfection to be suggested. The winter—with its snow and ice—is not an evil to be corrected. It is as it was designed and made to be—for the artist has had leisure to add beauty to use. My acquaintances—angels from the north. I had a vision thus prospectively of these birds as I stood in the swamps.

Pine grosbeak

December 12, 1859

The snow having come—we see where is the path of the partridge—his comings and goings from copse to copse. And now *first* as it were, we have the fox for our nightly neighbor—and countless tiny deer mice. So perchance if a still finer substance should fall from heaven (iodine?)—something delicate enough to receive the trace of their footsteps—we should see where unsuspected spirits and faery visitors had hourly crossed our steps, had held conventions and transacted their affairs in our midst. No doubt such subtle spirits transact their affairs in our midst and we may perhaps invent some sufficiently delicate surface—to catch the impression of them.

December 13, 1855

Sanborn tells me that he was waked up a few nights ago in Boston about midnight by the sound of a flock of geese passing over the city—probably about the same night I heard them here. They go honking over cities where the arts flourish—waking the inhabitants—over state-houses and capitols where legislatures sit—over harbors where fleets lie at anchor. Mistaking the city perhaps for a swamp or the edge of a lake—about settling in it, not suspecting that greater geese than they have settled there.

December 14, 1858

I see at Derby's shop a *barred* owl *Strix nebulosa* taken in the woods west of the factory on the 11th—found (with its wing broke) by a woodchopper. It measures *about* 3½ feet in alar extent by 18 to 20 inches long—or *nearly* the same as the cat owl—but is small and without horns. It is very mild and quiet—bears handling perfectly well—and only snaps its bill with a loud sound at the sight of a cat or dog. It is apparently a female since it is large—and has white spots on the wings. The claws are quite dark—rather than dark horn-color. It hopped into the basin of the scales—and I was surprised to find that it weighed only 1 lb and 1 oz. It may be thin fleshed on account of its broken wing—but how light-bodied these fliers are! It has no yellow iris like the cat owl—and has thin bristles about its yellow bill—which the other has not. It has a very smooth and handsome round head—a brownish gray.

Barred owl

Solemnity is what they express—fit representatives of the night.

December 15, 1855

How like a bird of ill omen the crow behaves! Still holding its ground in our midst like a powwow that is not to be exterminated! Sometimes when I am going through the Deep Cut—I look up and see half a dozen black crows flitting silently across in front and ominously eyeing down—passing from one wood to another—yet as if their passage had reference to me.

December 16, 1853

Some creature has killed ten, at least, of A. Wheeler's doves and left them together in the dove house. I think it was my short-eared owl which flew thither.

December 17, 1856

American woodcock

At Clamshell to my surprise scare up either a woodcock or a snipe. I think the former—for I plainly saw considerable red on the breast—also a light stripe along the neck. It was feeding alone close to the edge of the hill where it is springy and still soft—almost the only place of this character in the neighborhood—and though I started it three times, it each time flew but little way round to the hillside again—perhaps the same spot it had left a moment before—as if unwilling to leave this unfrozen and comparatively warm locality. It was a great surprise this bitter cold day—when so many springs were frozen up—to see this hardy bird loitering still. Once alighted—you could not see it till it arose again.

December 18, 1859

I see three shrikes—in different places today—two on the top of apple trees—sitting still in the storm on the lookout. They fly *low* to another tree when disturbed—much like a bluebird—and jerk their tails once or twice when they alight.

December 19, 1850

Yesterday I tracked a partridge in the new-fallen snow till I came to where she took to flight and I could track her no further.

December 20, 1855

A few chickadees busily inspecting the buds at the willow row—ivy tree—for insects—with a short clear chink from time to time, as if to warn me of their neighborhood.

December 21, 1851

As I stand by the edge of the swamp (Ministerial) a heavy-winged hawk flies home to it at sundown just over my head in silence.

Dark-eyed junco

December 22, 1858

I see in the cut near the shanty-site quite a flock
of *F. hyemalis* and goldfinches *together* on the snow and weeds
and ground. Hear the well-known mew and watery twitter of the last and the drier *chilt chilt* of the former. These burning yellow birds—with a little black and white on their coat flaps, look warm above the snow. There may be 30 goldfinches—very brisk and pretty tame. They hang head downwards on the weeds. I hear of their coming to pick sunflower seeds in Melvin's garden these days.

December 23, 1859

In this slight snow—I am surprised to see countless tracks of small birds which have run over it in every direction from one end to the other of this great meadow since morning. By the length of the hind toe I know them to be snow buntings (indeed soon after I see them running still on one side of the meadow). I was puzzled to tell what they got by running there. Yet stopping repeatedly and picking up something. Of course I thought of those caterpillars which are washed out by a freshet and rain at this season—but I could not find one of them. . . .

It is interesting to see how busy this flock is exploring this great meadow today. If it were not for this slight snow revealing their tracks, but hardly at all concealing the stubble, I should not suspect it, though

I might see them at their work. Now I see them running briskly over the ice—most commonly near the shore where there is most stubble (though *very little*)—and they explore the ground so fast that they were continually changing their ground—and if I do not keep my eye on them I lose the direction. Then here they come—with a stiff *rip* of their wings as they suddenly wheel and those peculiar *rippling* notes flying low quite across the meadow half a mile even, to explore the other side—though that too is already tracked by them. Not fisherman nor skater range the meadow a thousandth part so much in a week as these birds in a day. They hardly notice me as they come on. Indeed the flock flying about as high as my head divides and half passes on each side of me. Thus they sport over these broad meadows of ice this pleasant winter day. The spiders lie torpid and plain to see on the snow—and if it is they that they are after—they never know what kills them.

December 24, 1851

It spits snow this afternoon. Saw a flock of snowbirds on the Walden road. I see them so commonly when it is beginning to snow that I am inclined to regard them as a sign of a snowstorm. The snow bunting *Emberiza nivalis* [*Plectrophenax nivalis*] methinks it is—so white and arctic. Not the slate-colored. Saw also some pine grosbeaks—magnificent winter birds—among the weeds and on the apple trees—like large catbirds at a distance—but nearer at hand some of them when they flit by are seen to have gorgeous heads breasts and rumps (?) with red or crimson reflections—more beautiful than a steady bright red would be. The note I heard a rather faint and innocent whistle of two bars.

December 25, 1859

Standing by the side of the river at Eleazer Davis's Hill (prepared to pace across it) I hear a sharp fine *screep* from some bird—which at length I detect amid the buttonbushes and willows. The *screep* was a note of recognition meant for me. I saw that it was a novel bird to me. Watching it a long time with my glass and without it—I at length made out these marks. It was slate colored above and dirty white beneath—with a broad and very conspicuous bright orange crown—which in some lights was *red*-orange (along the middle of the head) this was bounded on each side by a black segment—beneath which was a yellow or whitish line. There was also some yellow and a black spot on the middle of the closed

Golden-crowned kinglet

wings—and yellow within the tail feathers. The ends of the wings and the tail above were *dusky* and the tail forked.

It was so very active that I could not get a steady view of it. It kept drifting about behind the stems of the buttonbushes etc.—half the time on the ice—and again on the lower twigs—busily looking for its prey—turning its body this way and that with great restlessness—appearing to hide from me behind the stems of the buttonbush and the withered coarse grass. When I came nearest it would utter its peculiar *screep*—or *screep screep* or even *screep screep screep*. Yet it was unwilling to leave the spot and when I cornered it—it hopped back within ten feet of me. However, I could see its brilliant crown even between the twigs of the buttonbush and through the withered grass when I could detect no other part.

It was evidently the golden-crested wren [golden-crowned kinglet]. Which I have not made out before.

This little creature was contentedly seeking its food here alone this cold winter day on the shore of our frozen river. If it does not visit us often—it is strange that it should choose such a season.

December 26, 1853

Walden still open. Saw in it a small diver probably a grebe or dobchick—dipper or whatnot—with the markings as far as I saw of the crested grebe but smaller. It had a black head—a white ring about its neck—a white breast—black back—and apparently no tail [horned grebe]. It dove and swam a few rods under water—and when on the surface kept turning round and round warily and nodding its head the while. This being the only pond hereabouts that is open.

Horned grebes

Black-capped chickadees

December 27, 1852

Not a particle of ice in Walden today. Paddled across it—and took my new boat out. A black and white duck on it. Flint's and Fair Haven being frozen up.

December 28, 1858

I notice a few chickadees there in the edge of the pines in the sun—lisping and twittering cheerfully to one another with a reference to me I think—the cunning and innocent little birds. One a little further off utters the *phebe* note. There is a foot more or less of clear open water at the edge here—and, seeing this one of these birds hops down as if glad to find any open water at this season—and after drinking—it stands in the water on a stone up to its belly—and dips its head and flirts the water about vigorously giving itself a good washing. I had not suspected this at this season. No fear that it will catch cold.

December 29, 1853

All day—a driving snowstorm imprisoning most—stopping the cars—blocking up the roads. No school today. I cannot see a house 50 rods off from my window through. . . . Yet in midst of all I see a bird—probably a tree sparrow—partly blown partly flying over the house to alight in a field. . . .

What a contrast between the village street now and last summer. The leafy elms then resounding with the warbling vireo—robins, bluebirds, and the fiery hangbird [Baltimore oriole] etc.—to which the villagers kept indoors by the heat listen through open lattices. Now it is like a street in Nova Zembla—if they were to have any there. . . .

Of the snow bunting—Wilson says that they appear in the northern parts of the US "early in December, or with the first heavy snow, particularly if drifted by high winds." This day answers to that description exactly. . . . Peabody says that in summer they are "pure white and black" but are not seen of that color here. Those I saw today were of that color behind A. Wheeler's. He says they are white and rusty brown here.

These are the true winter birds for you, these winged snowballs. I could hardly see them the air was so full of driving snow. What hardy creatures. Where do they spend the night?

December 30, 1859

P.M. Going by Dodd's—I see a shrike perched on the tip-top of the topmost upright twig of an English cherry tree before his house. Standing square on the topmost bud—balancing himself by a slight motion of his tail from time to time. I have noticed this habit of the bird before. You would suppose it inconvenient for so large a bird to maintain its footing there. Scared by my passing in the road—it flew off and I thought I would see if it alighted on a similar place. It flew toward a young elm, whose higher twigs were much more slender though not quite so upright as those of the cherry, and I thought he might be excused if he alighted on the side of one—but no, to my surprise he alighted without any trouble upon the very top of one of the highest of all—and looked around as before. . . .

I noticed the other day that even the golden-crested wren was one of the winter birds which have a black head (in this case divided by yellow).

December 31, 1859

Crows yesterday flitted silently, if not ominously over the street—just after the snow had fallen—as if men being further within—were just as far off as usual. This is a phenomenon of both cold weather and snowy. You hear nothing, you merely see these black apparitions, though they come near enough to look down your chimney and scent the boiling pot—and pass between the house and barn.

JANUARY

January 1, 1854

The Indians might have imagined a large snow bunting to be the genius of the storm.

January 2, 1854

Took a walk on snowshoes at 9 A.M. to Hubbard's Grove. A flock of snow buntings flew over the fields with a rippling whistle accompanied sometimes by a tender peep and a ricochet motion.

January 3, 1860

Saw four snow buntings by the railroad causeway just this side the cut—quite tame. They arose and alighted on the rail fence as we went by—very stout for their length. Look very pretty when they fly and reveal the clear white space on their wings next the body—white between the blacks. They were busily eating the seed of the piper grass on the embankment there and it was strewn over the snow by them like oats in a stable. Melvin speaks of seeing flocks of them on the river meadows in the fall—when they are of a different color.

Snow buntings

January 4, 1859

When it grew late—the air being thick and unelastic in this storm—I mistook the distant sound of the locomotive whistle for the hoot of an owl. It was quite like it.

I see nevertheless a few tree sparrows about—looking chubbier than ever—their feathers being puffed up—and flitting and twittering merrily along the fence.

January 5, 1860

How much the snow reveals! I see where the downy woodpecker has worked lately—by the chips of bark and rotten wood scattered over the snow—though I rarely see him in the winter. Once today however I hear his sharp voice—even like a woodchuck's.

Also I have occasionally seen where (probably) a flock of goldfinches in the morning had settled on a hemlock top—by the snow strewn with scales—literally blackened or darkened with them for a rod.

And now about the hill in front of Smith's I see where the quails have run along the roadside—I can count the number of the bevy better than if I saw them.

Are they not peculiar in this as compared with partridges—that they run in company—while at this season I see but [one] or two partridges together?

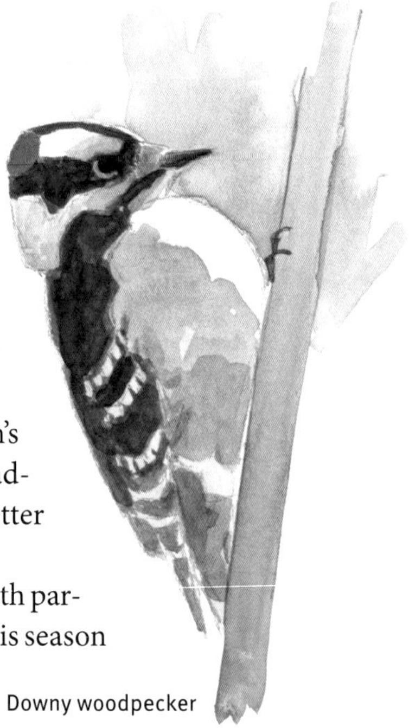

Downy woodpecker

January 6, 1859

Miles had hanging in his barn a little owl (*Strix Acadica*) [saw-whet owl] which he caught alive with his hands about a week ago. He had forced it to eat—but it died. It was a funny little brown bird—spotted with white 7½ inches long to the end of the tail—or eight to the end of the claws—by 19 in alar extent—but not so long by considerable as a robin though much stouter. This one had three (not two) white bars on its tail—but no noticeable white at the tip. Its curving feet were feathered quite to the extremity of the toes—looking like whitish (or tawny white) mice—or as when one pulls stockings over his boots. As usual, the white spots on the upper sides of the wings are smaller and a more distinct white—while those beneath are much larger but a subdued, satiny white. Even a bird's wing has an upper and under side—and the last admits only of more subdued and tender colors.

January 7, 1860

Saw a large flock of goldfinches—running and feeding amid the weeds in a pasture—just like tree sparrows. Then flitted to birch trees, whose seeds *probably* they eat. Heard their twitter and mew. So it is possible that they also eat hemlock seed.

American goldfinch

January 8, 1855

It is now a clear warm and sunny day. The willow osiers by the Red Bridge decidedly are not bright now. There is a healthy earthy sound of cock-crowing. I hear a few chickadees near at hand—and hear and see jays further off—and as yesterday—a crow sitting sentinel on an apple tree. Soon he gives the alarm and several more take their places near him. Then off they flap with their "caw" of various hoarseness.

January 9, 1859

The sun has been set some minutes and as I stand on the pond looking westward toward the twilight sky—a soft satiny light is reflected from the ice in flakes here and there like the light from the underside of a bird's wing.

January 10, 1859

See, returning, amid the *Roman wormwood* in front of the Monroe place—by the river half a dozen goldfinches feeding just like the sparrows. How warm their yellow breasts look. They utter the goldfinches' watery twitter still.

January 11, 1856

Mother reminds me that when we lived at the Parkman House she lost a ruff 1½ yards long and with an edging three yards long to it which she had laid on the grass to whiten—and looking for it she saw a robin tugging at the tape string of a stay on the line. He would repeatedly get it in his mouth—fly off and be brought up when he got to the end of his tether. Miss Ward thereupon tore a fine linen handkerchief into strips and threw them out—and the robin carried them all off. She had no doubt that he took the ruff.

January 12, 1859

Mr. Farmer brings me a hawk—which he thinks has caught 30 or 40 of his chickens since summer—for he has lost so many—and he has seen a hawk like this catch some of them. Thinks he has seen this same one sitting a long time upright on a tree high or low about his premises—and when at length a hen or this year's chicken had strayed far from the rest it skimmed along and picked her up without pausing and bore her off—the chicken not having seen him approaching. He found this caught by one leg and frozen to death in a trap which he had set for mink by a spring—and baited with fish.

This measures 19 by 42 inches and is according to Wilson and Nuttall a *young F. lineatus* or red-shouldered hawk. It might as well be called red or rusty-breasted hawk. Nuttall says it

Red-shouldered hawk

lives on frogs—crayfish—etc. and does not go far north—not even to Massachusetts he thought. Its note *kee-oo.*

January 13, 1860

One man at the P.O. said that a crow would drive a fox. He had seen three crows pursue a fox that was crossing the Great Meadows, and he fairly ran from and took refuge in the woods.

January 14, 1852

When I see the dead stems of the tansy—goldenrod—johnswort—asters—hardhack etc. etc. rising above the snow by the roadside, sometimes in dense masses, which carry me back in imagination to their green summer life, I put faintly a question which I do not yet hear answered—why stand they there? Why should the dead cornstalks occupy the field longer than the green and living did? Many of them are granaries for the birds.

January 15, 1857

Song sparrow

As I passed the south shed at the depot—observed what I thought a tree sparrow on the wood in the shed—a mere roof open at the side—under which several men were at that time employed sawing wood with a horse-power. Looking closer I saw, to my surprise, that it must be a song sparrow it having the usual marks on its breast and no bright chestnut crown. The snow is nine or ten inches deep and it appeared to have taken refuge in this shed where was much bare ground exposed by removing the wood. When I advanced, instead of flying away, it concealed itself in the wood, just as it often dodges behind a wall.

January 16, 1860

I see a flock of tree sparrows busily picking something from the surface of the snow amid some bushes. I watch one attentively, and find that it is feeding on the very fine brown chaffy-looking seed of the panicled andromeda.

It understands how to get its dinner—to make the plant *give down*, perfectly. It flies up and alights on one of the dense brown panicles of the hard berries—and gives it a vigorous shaking and beating with its claws and bill—sending down a shower of the fine chaffy-looking seed on to the snow beneath. It lies very distinct though fine almost as dust, on the spotless snow. It then hops down and briskly picks up from the snow what it wants. How very clean and agreeable to the imagination and withal abundant is this kind of food! How delicately they fare! These dry persistent seed vessels hold their crusts of bread—until shaken. The snow is the white table cloth on which they fall. No anchorite with his water and his crust fares more simply. It shakes down a hundred times as much as it wants at each shrub and shakes the same or another cluster after each successive snow.

January 17, 1856

Henry Shattuck tells me that the quails come almost every day and get some saba beans within two or three rods of his house. Some which he neglected to gather. Probably the deep snow drives them to it.

January 18, 1859

Two or more inches of snow fell last night. In the expanse this side Mantatuket Rock I see the tracks of a crow or crows in and about the buttonbushes and willows. They have trampled and pecked much in some spots under the buttonbushes where these seeds are still left and dibbled into the snow by them. It would seem then that they eat them. The only other seeds there can be there are those of the mikania—for I look for them. You will see a crow's track beginning in the middle of the river—where one alighted.

I notice such a track as this where one alighted and apparently stuck its spread tail into the snow—at the same time with its feet. I see afterward where a wing's quills have marked the snow much like a partridge's. The snow is very light—so that the tracks are rarely distinct—and as they often advance by hops some might mistake it for a squirrel's or mink's track. I suspect that they came here yesterday after minnows—when the fishermen were gone—and that has brought

them here today in spite of the snow. They evidently look out sharp for a morsel of fish.

I see where by the red maple above Pinxter Swamp they have picked over the fine dark greenish moss from buttonbush and the leaves which had formed a squirrel's nest—knocking it down on to the river—and there treading about and pecking a small piece—apparently for some worms or insects that were in it—as if they were hard pushed.

January 19, 1855

At noon it is still a driving snowstorm—and a little flock of redpolls is busily picking the seeds of the pigweed etc. in the garden. Almost all have more or less crimson—a few are very splendid with their particularly bright crimson breasts. The white on the edge of their wing coverts is very conspicuous.

January 20, 1860

The snow and ice under the hemlocks is strewn with cones and seeds—and tracked with birds and squirrels. What a bountiful supply of winter food is here provided for them. No sooner has fresh snow fallen and covered up the old crop—than down comes a new supply all the more distinct on the spotless snow. Here comes a little flock of chickadees, attracted by me as usual—and perching close by boldly. Then descending to the snow and ice I see them pick at the hemlock seed which lies all around them. Occasionally they take one to a twig and hammer at it there under their claws perhaps to separate it from the wing—or even

Common redpoll

the shell. The snowy ice—and the snow on shore have been blackened with these fallen cones several times over this winter.

The snow along the sides of the river is also all dusted over with birch and alder seed. I see where little birds have picked up the alder seed.

January 21, 1857

Minott tells me that Sam Barrett told him—once when he went to mill that a song sparrow took up its quarters in his grist mill and stayed there all winter. When it did not help itself he used to feed it with meal—for he was glad of its company—so what with the dashing water and the crumbs of meal—it must have fared well.

January 22, 1856

Somebody has been fishing in the pond this morning and the water in the holes is beginning to freeze. I see the track of a crow the toes as usual less spread—and the middle one making a more curved furrow in the snow than the partridge—as if they moved more unstably recovering their balance—feeble on their feet. The inner toe a little the nearest to the middle one. This track goes to every hole but one or two out of a dozen (directly from hole to hole sometimes flying a little)—and also to an apple core on the snow. I am pretty sure that this bird was after the bait which is usually dropped on the ice or in the hole. E. Garfield says they come regularly to his holes for bait as soon as he has left. So if the pickerel are not fed it is. It had even visited, on the wing, a hole now frozen and snowed up which I made far from this in the middle of the pond several days since—as I discovered by its droppings. The same kind that it had left about the first holes.

January 23, 1852

The snow is so deep and the cold so intense that the crows are compelled to be very bold in seeking their food—and come very near the houses in the village. One is now walking about and pecking the dung in the street in front of Frank Monroe's. They remind me as they sail along over the street of the turkey buzzards [turkey vultures] of the south and perhaps many hard winters in succession would make them as tame.

January 24, 1856

I knew that a crow had that day plucked the cedar berries and barberries by Flint's Pond—and then flapped silently through the trackless air to Walden, where it dined on fisherman's bait—though there was no living creature to tell me. . . .

Here are the tracks of a crow like those of the 22d—with a *long hind toe* nearly two inches. The two feet are also nearly two inches apart. I see where the bird alighted descending with an impetus and breaking through the slight crust planting its feet side by side.

How different this partridge track with its slight hind toe—open and wide-spread toes on each side—both feet forming one straight line, exactly thus. (Five inches from center to center.) The middle toe alternately curved to the right and to the left—and, what is apparently the outer toe, in each case shorter than the inner one.

Ruffed grouse in snow

January 25, 1855

In the partridge tracks the side toes are more spread than in crows and I believe the hind one is not so long—both trail the middle toe. The partridge track looks like this.

I see the tracks apparently of many hunters that hastened out this morning.

January 26, 1852

The woodpeckers work in Emerson's wood on the cliff-top, the trees being partly killed by the top, and the grubs having hatched under the bark. The woodpeckers have stripped a whole side of some trees—and in a sound red oak they have dug out a mortise hole with squarish shoulders as if with a chisel. I have often seen these holes.

January 27, 1860

Half a dozen redpolls busily picking the seeds out of the larch cones behind Monroe's. They are pretty tame—and I stood near. They perch on the slender twigs which are beaded with cones—and swing and teeter there while they persevering peck at them trying now this one, now that, and sometimes appearing to pick out and swallow them quite fast. I notice no redness or carmine at first—but when the top of one's head comes between me and the sun it unexpectedly glows.

January 28, 1858

Minott has a sharp ear for the note of any migrating bird. Though confined to his dooryard by the rheumatism he commonly hears them sooner than the widest rambler. Maybe he listens all day for them—or they come and sing over his house—report themselves to him and receive their season ticket. He is never at fault. If he says he heard such a bird—though sitting by his chimney side you may depend on it. He can swear through glass. He has not spoiled his ears by attending lectures or caucuses etc. The other day the rumor went that a flock of geese had been seen flying north over Concord (midwinter as it was by the almanac). I traced it to Minott and yet I was compelled to doubt. I had it directly that he had heard them within a week. I saw him—I made haste to him. His reputation was at stake. He said that he stood in his shed—it was one of the late warm muggy April-like mornings—when he heard one short but distinct *honk* of a goose. He went into the house, he took his cane—he exerted himself—or that sound imparted strength to *him*. Lame as he was he went up on to the hill—he had not done it for a year—that he might hear all around. He saw nothing, but he heard the note—again. It came from over the brook. It was a wild goose—he was sure of it. And hence the rumor spread and grew. He thought that the back of the winter was broken—if it had any this year—but he feared such a winter would kill him too.

I was silent—I reflected—I drew into my mind all its members—like the tortoise—I abandoned myself to unseen guides. Suddenly the truth flashed on me—and I *remembered* that within a week I had heard of a box at the tavern which had come by railroad express containing three wild geese and directed to his neighbor over the brook. The April-like morning had excited one so that he honked. And Minott's reputation acquired new luster.

January 29, 1860

Not only the Indian, but many wild birds and quadrupeds and insects welcomed the apple tree to these shores. As it grew apace the bluebird—robin—cherry bird, kingbird, and many more came with a rush and built their nests in its boughs and so became orchard birds.

The woodpecker found such a savory morsel under its bark—that he perforated it in a ring quite round the tree—a thing he had never done before. It did not take the partridge long to find out how sweet its buds were, and every winter day she flew and still flies from the wood—to pluck them much to the farmer's sorrow. The rabbit too was not slow to learn the taste of its twigs and bark. The owl crept into the first one that became hollow—and fairly hooted with delight—finding it just the place for him. He settled down into it, and has remained there ever since.

The lackey caterpillar saddled her eggs on the very first twig that was found—and it has since divided her affections with the wild cherry—and the canker worm also in a measure abandoned the elm to feed on it.

And when the fruit was ripe the squirrel half carried half rolled it to his hole—and even the musquash crept up the bank and greedily devoured it—and when it was frozen and thawed the crow and jay did not disdain to peck it. And the beautiful wood duck—having made up her mind to stay a while longer with us—has concluded that there is no better place for her too.

January 30, 1860

Crows have singular wild and suspicious ways—you will [see] a couple flying high as if about their business—but as they turn and circle and caw over your head again and again for a mile—and this is their business—as if a mile and an afternoon were nothing for them to throw away. This even in winter when they have no nest to be anxious about.

But it is affecting to hear them cawing about their ancient seat (as at F. Wheeler's wood) which the choppers are laying low.

January 31, 1854

Many tracks of partridges there along the meadowside in the maples—and their droppings where they appear to have spent the night about the roots and between the stems of trees. I think they eat the buds of the azalea. And now with a mew preluding a whir they go off before me. Coming up I follow her tracks to where she eased herself for lightness—and immediately after are five or six parallel cuts in the snow where her wing struck when she lifted herself from the ground—but no trace more.

FEBRUARY

February 1, 1856

Nut Meadow Brook open for some distance in the meadow. . . . I see where a crow has walked along its side. In one place it hopped—and its feet were side by side as in the track of yesterday—though a little more spread the toes. I have but little doubt that yesterday's track was a crow's.

The two inner toes are near together—the middle more or less curved often. . . . The crows have been remarkably bold coming to eat the scraps cast out behind the houses. They alight in our yard.

February 2, 1858

Still rains after a rainy night with a little snow—forming slosh. As I return from the P.O. I hear the hoarse robin-like chirp of a song sparrow on Cheney's ground—and see him perched on the topmost twig of a heap of brush—looking forlorn and drabbled and solitary in the rain.

February 3, 1856

Returning saw near the Island a shrike glide by, cold and blustering as it was—with a remarkably even and steady sail or gliding motion like a hawk—eight or ten feet above the ground and alight on a tree from which at the same instant a small bird—perhaps a creeper or nut-hatch flitted timidly away. The shrike was apparently in pursuit.

Song sparrow

Northern shrike

February 4, 1856

I see that the partridges feed quite extensively on the sumac berries—e.g. at my old house. They come to them after every snow—making fresh tracks and have now stripped many bushes quite bare. . . .

I have often wondered how red cedars could have sprung up in some pastures which I knew to be miles distant from the nearest fruit-bearing cedar—but it now occurs to me that these and barberries etc. may be planted by the crows—and probably other birds.

February 5, 1860

I see where crows have pecked the tufts of cladonia lichens which peep out of the snow—pulling them to pieces—no doubt looking for worms. Also have eaten the frozen thawed apples under the trees—tracking all the ground over there.

February 6, 1856

Goodwin says that he has caught two crows this winter in his traps set *in water* for mink, and baited with fish. The crows probably put to it for food and looking along the very few open brooks attracted by this bait got their feet into the traps.

February 7, 1855

Two frog hawks [northern harriers] (white rump—and slaty wings rather small hawk) have their nest regularly at his place [R. Rice] in Sudbury. He once saw one—the male he thinks—come along from the meadow with a frog in his claws. As he flew up toward and over the wood where the other was setting—he uttered a peculiar cry and the other darting out he let the frog drop two or three rods through the air which the other caught.

February 8, 1841

My Journal is that of me which would else spill over and run to waste—gleanings from the field which in action I reap. I must not live for it, but in it for the gods. They are my correspondent to whom daily I send off this sheet post-paid. I am clerk in their counting room and at evening transfer the account from daybook to ledger.

It is as a leaf which hangs over my head in the path—I bend the twig and write my prayers on it then letting it go the bough springs up and shows the scrawl to heaven. As if it were not kept shut in my desk—but were as public a leaf as any in nature. It is papyrus by the riverside—it is vellum in the pastures—it is parchment on the hills. I find it everywhere as free as the leaves which troop along the lanes in autumn. The crow—the goose—the eagle carry my quill—and the wind blows the leaves—as far as I go. Or if my imagination does not soar, but gropes in slime and mud—then I write with a reed.

February 9, 1854

I do not hear Therien's axe far of late. The moment I came on his chopping ground the chickadees flew to me—as if glad to see me. They are a peculiarly honest and sociable little bird. I saw them go to his pail repeatedly and peck his bread and butter. They came and went a dozen times while I stood there. He said that a great flock of them came round him the other day—while he was eating his dinner and lit on his clothes "just like flies." One roosted on his finger and another pecked a piece of bread in his hand. They are considerable company for the woodchopper. I heard one wiry *phebe*. They love to hop about wood freshly split. Apparently they do not leave his clearing all day. They were not scared when he threw down wood within a few feet of them. When I looked to see how much of his bread and butter they had eaten—I did not perceive that any was gone. He could afford to dine a hundred of them.

February 10, 1855

I hear the faint metallic chirp of a tree sparrow in the yard from time to time—or perchance the mew of a linaria. It is worth the while to let some pigweed grow in your garden if only to attract these winter visitors. It would be a pity to have these weeds burned in the fall. Of the former I see in the winter but three or four commonly at a time—of the latter large flocks. This in and after considerable snowstorms.

February 11, 1855

The atmosphere is very blue tingeing the distant pine woods. The dog scared up some partridges out of the soft snow under the apple trees in the Tommy Wheeler orchard.

February 12, 1855

I see at Warren's Crossing where last night perhaps some partridges rested in this light dry deep snow. They must have been almost completely buried. They have left their traces at the bottom. They are such holes as would be made by crowding their bodies in backwards slantingwise—while perhaps their heads were left out. The dog scared them out of similar holes yesterday in the open orchard. . . .

Under the birches, where the snow is covered with birch seeds and scales, I see the fine tracks undoubtedly of linarias. The track of one of these birds in the light surface looks like a chain or the ova of toads. Where a large flock has been feeding the whole surface is scored over by them.

February 13, 1855

The tracks of partridges are more remarkable in this snow than usual—it is so light—being at the same time a foot deep. I see where one has waddled along several rods making a chain-like track about 3 inches wide (or 2½) and at the end has squatted in the snow making a perfectly smooth and regular oval impression like the bowl of a spoon five inches wide. Then six inches beyond this are the marks of its wings where it struck the snow on each side when it took flight. It must have risen at once without running. In one place I see where one after running a little way—has left four impressions of its wings on the snow on each side extending 18 or 20 inches and 12 or 15 in width.

February 14, 1851

One afternoon in the fall November 21st I saw Fair Haven Pond with its island and meadow between the island and the shore, a strip of perfectly smooth water in the lee of the island and two hawks sailing over it (and something more I saw which cannot easily be described which made me say to myself that it, the landscape could not be improved). I did not see how it could be improved. Yet I do not know what these things can be; I begin to see such objects only when I leave off understanding them—and afterwards remember that I did not appreciate them before. But I get no further than this. How adapted these forms and colors to our eyes, a meadow and its islands. What are these things? Yet the hawks and the ducks keep so aloof, and nature is so reserved! We are made to love the river and the meadow as the wind to ripple the water.

February 15, 1841

The moments will be outspread around us like a blue expanse of mountain and valley, while we stand on the summit of our hour as if we had descended on eagle's wings. For the eagle has stooped to his perch on the highest cliff—and has never climbed the rock. He stands by his wings more than his feet. We shall not want a foothold, but wings will sprout from our shoulders, and we shall walk securely self-sustained.

February 16, 1855

I find in the leavings of the partridges numerous ends of twigs. They are white with them—some ½ inch long and stout in proportion. Perhaps they are apple twigs? The bark (and bud if there was any) has been entirely digested leaving the bare white hard wood of the twig. Some of the ends of apple twigs looked as if they had been bitten off. It is surprising what a quantity of this wood they swallow with their buds. What a hardy bird—born amid the dry leaves—of the same color with them—that grown up lodges in the snow—and lives on buds and twigs!

Where apple buds are just freshly bitten off they do not seem to have taken so much twig with them.

February 17, 1855

Heard this morn at the new stone bridge from the hill that singular spring-like note of a bird which I heard once before one year about this time (under Fair Haven Hill). The jays were uttering their unusual notes—and this made me think of a woodpecker. It reminds me of the pine warbler—*vetter vetter vetter vetter vet*—except that it is much louder—and I should say had the sound of l rather than t—*veller* etc. perhaps. Can it be a jay? Or a pigeon woodpecker? Is it not the earliest springward note of a bird? In the damp misty air.

February 18, 1854

At the old mill-site saw two pigeon woodpeckers dart into and out of a white oak. Saw the yellow undersides of their wings. It is barely possible I am mistaken—but since Wilson makes them common in Pennsylvania in winter—I feel pretty sure. Such sights make me think there must be bare ground not far off south.

February 19, 1857

Mr. Cheney tells me that Goodwin brought him a partridge to sell in the midst of the late severe weather. C. said it was a pity to kill it—it must find it hard to get a living. "I guess she didn't find it any harder than I do" answered G.

February 20, 1859

P.M. I see directly in front the Depot ice house, on the only piece of *bare ground I see hereabouts* a large flock of lesser redpolls feeding. They must be picking up earth sand or the withered grass. They are so intent on it that they allow me to come quite near.

This then is one use for the drifting of snow which lays bare some spots—however deep it may be elsewhere, so that the birds etc. can come at the earth. I never thought of this use before. First the snow fell deep and level on the 18th then the 19th, came high wind and plowed it out here and there to the ground, and so it will always be in *some* places however deep it may have been.

Common redpolls

February 21, 1855

Can it be true, as is said, that geese have gone over Boston probably yesterday? It is in the newspapers.

February 22, 1855

Remarkably warm and pleasant weather—perfect spring. I even listen for the first bluebird. I see a seething in the air over clean russet fields.

February 23, 1859

I first hear and then see 8 or 10 bluebirds going over. Perhaps they have not reached Concord yet. One boy tells me that he saw a bluebird in Concord on Sunday *the 20th*.

Eastern bluebird (female)

February 24, 1854

In Wheeler's Wood by railroad. Nuthatches are faintly answering each other—tit for tat—on different keys (a faint creak). Now and then one utters a loud distinct *gnah*. This bird more than any I know loves to stand with its head downward.

Meanwhile chickadees with their silver tinkling are flitting high above through the tops of the pines.... Observed in one of the little pond holes between Walden and Fair Haven where a partridge had traveled around in the snow amid the bordering bushes 25 rods—had pecked the green leaves of the lambkill and left fragments on the snow—and had paused at each high blueberry bush, fed on its red buds and shaken down fragments of its bark on the snow. These buds appeared its main object. I finally scared the bird.

February 25, 1859

Measure your health by your sympathy with morning and spring. If there is no response in you to the awakening of nature—if the prospect of an early morning walk does not banish sleep—if the warble of the first bluebird does not thrill you—know that the morning and spring of your life are past.

Thus may you feel your pulse.

February 26, 1856

In Hubbard's maple swamp beyond I see the snow within a few days sprinkled with the sawdust like bits of wood under a dead maple where a woodpecker has drilled a handsome round hole. Excepting the carrying it downward within it is ready for a nest. May they not have a view to this use even now?

February 27, 1860

I had noticed for some time far in the middle of the Great Meadows something dazzlingly white—which I took of course to be a small cake of ice on its end—but now that I have climbed the pitch pine hill and can overlook the whole meadow—I see it to be the white breast of a male sheldrake accompanied perhaps by his mate (a darker one). They have settled warily in the very midst of the meadow—where the wind has blown a space of clear water for an acre or two. The aspect of the meadow is sky blue—and dark blue—the former a thin ice—the latter the spaces of open water which the wind has made—but it is chiefly ice still. Thus as soon as the river breaks up—or begins to break up fairly—and the strong wind widening the cracks makes at length open spaces in the ice of the meadow—this hardy bird appears and is seen sailing in the first widened crack in the ice where it can come at the water. Instead of a piece of ice—I find it to be the breast of the sheldrake which so reflects the light as to look larger than it is, steadily sailing this way and that with its companion who is diving from time to time. They have chosen the opening farthest removed from all shores. As I look I see the ice drifting in upon them and contracting their water—till finally they have but a few square rods left, while there are 40 or 50 acres nearby. This is the first bird of the spring that I have seen or heard of.

February 28, 1855

Found a hangbird's nest fallen from the ivy maple—composed wholly of that thread they wipe the locomotive with—"cotton waste"—and one real thread all as it were woven into a perfect bag.

THE PASSENGER PIGEON

APPENDIX A

When Thoreau died in 1862, few people suspected that the passenger pigeon was on the road to extinction. Yet barely fifty years later, in 1914, the last known passenger pigeon in the world died at the Cincinnati Zoo. Her name was Martha.

Even so, Thoreau seemed to sense that the days of endless flocks of passenger pigeons were passing away. As early as 1845 he called them "an ancient race of birds." In 1850, he mentioned "the old pigeon place field by the Deep Cut," a grassy field that had grown up into woodland. Seeing an active pigeon place at "George Heywood's cleared lot" with six dead trees set up as pigeon roosts and a blind made of brush, he wrote, "I was rather startled to find such a thing going now in Concord. The pigeons on the tree looked like fabulous birds with their long tails and their pointed breasts." In 1852, he saw some pigeons in the woods, "with their inquisitive necks and long tails, but few representatives of the great flocks that once broke down our forests." In 1857, he wrote, "The very fishes in countless schools are driven out of a river by the *improvements* of the civilized man, as the pigeon and other fowls out of the air."

March 21, 1840

The wild goose is more a cosmopolite than we—he breaks his fast in Canada—takes a luncheon in the Susquehanna—and plumes himself for the night in a Louisiana bayou. The pigeon carries an acorn in his crop from the King of Holland's to Mason and Dixon's line. Yet we think if rail fences are pulled down and stone walls set up on our farms—bounds are henceforth set to our lives and our fates decided.

1842–1844

The neighboring wood was alive with pigeons which were now moving south looking for mast—like ourselves spending their noon in the shade. It is pleasant to stand in the oak or white pine woods and hear the slight wiry winnowing sound of their wings—and their gentle tremulous cooing. You will frequently discover a single pair in the depths of the wood, sitting upon the lower branches of the white pine, at noon. So silent and motionless and with such a hermit-like appearance as if they had never strayed beyond the skirts of the forest—while the acorn which was gathered in the woods of Maine is not yet digested in their crop.

July 16, 1845

"How thick the pigeons are" said he [Therien], "if working every day were not my trade I could get all the meat I should want by hunting. Pigeons—woodchucks—rabbits—partridges—by George I could get all I should want for a week in one day."

August 6, 1845

I sit here at my window like a priest of Isis—and observe the phenomena of three thousand years ago, yet unimpaired. The tantivy of wild pigeons, an ancient race of birds, gives a voice to the air—flying by twos and threes athwart my view or perching restless on the white pine boughs occasionally. A fish hawk dimples the glassy surface of the pond and brings up a fish. And for the last half hour I have heard the rattle of railroad cars conveying travelers from Boston to the country.

Fall–Winter 1845–1846

The passage of wild pigeons from this wood to that—with their slight tantivy—and carrier haste. Now from under some rotten stump your hoe turns up a spotted salamander—your own contemporary. A small trace of Egypt and the Nile in New England. Where is the priest of Isis.

After May 31, 1850

The fire now reached the base of the cliffs and then rushed up its sides. The squirrels ran before it in blind haste and the pigeons dashed into the midst of the smoke. The flames flashed up the pines to their tops as if they were powder.

November 9, 1850

There was the old Kettell place—now Watt's which I surveyed for him last winter and lotted off—where 25 years ago I played horse in the paths of a thick wood and roasted apples and potatoes in an old pigeon place—and gathered fruit at the pie-apple tree. . . . There is also the old pigeon place field by the Deep Cut. I remember it as an open grassy field. It is now one of our most pleasant woodland paths.

November 14, 1850

Saw today while surveying in the Second Division woods a singular round mound in a valley made perhaps 60 or 70 years ago. Cyrus Stow thought it was a pigeon bed—but I soon discovered the coal and that it was an old coal bed.

June 11, 1851

When I rose out of the Deep Cut into the old pigeon place field, I rose into a warmer stratum of air it being lighter. It told of the day, of sunny noontide hours, an air in which work had been done—which men had breathed.

July 21, 1851

Some pigeons here are resting in the thickest of the white pines during the heat of the day—migrating no doubt. They are unwilling to move for me. Flies buzz and rain about my hat—and the dead twigs and leaves of the white pine which the choppers have left here exhale a dry and almost sickening scent. A cuckoo chuckles half throttled on a neighboring tree—and now flying into the pine scares out a pigeon which flies with its handsome tail spread, dashes this side and that between the trees helplessly like a ship carrying too much sail in midst of a small creek, some great ammiral—having no room to maneuver. A fluttering flight.

August 17, 1851

I am not so poor. I can smell the ripening apples—the very rills are deep—the autumnal flowers, the *Trichostema dichotomum* [forked bluecurls]—not only its bright blue flower above the sand but its strong wormwood scent which belongs to the season feed my spirit—endear the earth to me—make me value myself and rejoice. The quivering of pigeons' wings—reminds me of the tough fiber of the air which they rend.

September 12, 1851

Saw a pigeon place on George Heywood's cleared lot—the six dead trees set up for the pigeons to alight on, and the brush house close by to conceal the man. I was rather startled to find such a thing going now in Concord. The pigeons on the tree looked like fabulous birds with their long tails and their pointed breasts. I could hardly believe they were alive and not some wooden birds used for decoys—they sat so still—and even when they moved their necks I thought it was the effect of art. As they were not catching them I approached and scared away a dozen birds who were perched in the trees and found that they were freshly baited there—though the net was carried away—perchance to some other bed. . . . As I stood there I heard a rushing sound and looking up saw a flock of 30 or 40 pigeons dashing toward the *trees*, who suddenly whirled on seeing me and circled round and made a new dash toward the bed as if they would fain alight if I had not been there—then steered off. I went into the bough house and lay awhile looking through the leaves—hoping to see them come again and feed—but they did not while I stayed. This net and bed belongs to one Harrington of Weston as I hear. Several men still take pigeons in Concord every year. By a method methinks extremely old and which I seem to have seen pictured in some old books of fables or symbols—and yet few in Concord know exactly how it is done. And yet it is all done for money and because the birds fetch a good price—just as the farmers raise corn and potatoes. I am always expecting that those engaged in such a pursuit will be somewhat less groveling and mercenary than the regular trader or farmer, but I fear that it is not so.

October 8, 1851

How easily at this season I could feed myself in the woods! There is mast for me too—as well as for the pigeon—and the squirrel. This Dodonean fruit.

October 19, 1851

Observed an oak—a red or black—at a pigeon place—whose top limbs were cut off perhaps a month ago; the leaves had dried a sort of snuff-yellow and rather glossy.

February 13, 1852

The actual bee-hunter—and pigeon-catcher—is familiar with facts in the natural history of bees and pigeons—which Huber and even Audubon are totally ignorant of. I love best the unscientific man's knowledge, there is so much more humanity in it. It is connected with true *sports*.

April 25, 1852

Found in the midst of the woods in Acton, on the Concord line a small shanty or shed whitewashed—which I mistook at first through the trees for a white marble tomb—with a slight clearing about it. Is it a bowling alley? Is it a pigeon place?

May 9, 1852

Saw pigeons in the woods with their inquisitive necks and long tails—but few representatives of the great flocks that once broke down our forests.

May 17, 1852

Methinks they were turtle doves which I saw this afternoon baited to a pigeon place—they fly like a pigeon, a slender darting bird. I do not surely know them apart.

May 22, 1852

On my way to Plymouth looked at Audubon in the State House. Saw painted the *red* berries of the *Arum triphyllum* [Jack-in-the-pulpit]. The pigeon is more red on the breast and more blue than the turtle dove.

The female (and male?) wood thrush spotted the whole length of belly; the hermit thrush not so. The seringo bird cannot be the Savannah sparrow.

June 10, 1852

Froth on the pigeon plain pines.

June 15, 1852

Ascending to pigeon place plain. The reflection of the heat from the dead pine needles and the boughs strewn about—combined with the dry suffocating scent is oppressive and reminds me of the first settlers of Concord.

September 2, 1852

Small flocks of pigeons are seen these days. Distinguished from doves by their sharper wings and bodies.

March 29, 1853

He [Elisha Dugan] saw two pigeons today—*prated* for them. They came near and then flew away.

August 11, 1853

The shadow of an elm stretches quite across the meadow. I see pigeons (?) in numbers fly up from the stubble.

September 2, 1853

Hear the sharp *quivet* of pigeons at the Thrush Alley clearing—mistook it for a jay at first—but saw the narrow swift flying bird soon.

December 15, 1853

He [George Brooks] had ten live pigeons in a cage under his barn—he used them to attract others in the spring. The reflections from their necks were very beautiful. They made me think of shells cast up on a beach. He placed them in a cage on the bed and could hear them prate at the house. Are we not all wreckers contriving that some treasure may be washed up on our beach and we may secure it—and do we not contract the habits of wreckers from the common modes of getting a living? The turtle doves plagued him for they were restless and frightened the pigeons.

March 7, 1854

Saw mountain cranberry near Brooks' pigeon place very flat on the pasture raying out from a center six feet each way, more than ¾ of an inch thick in the middle.

March 19, 1854

Goodwin killed a pigeon yesterday.

April 25, 1854

I think I saw a pigeon yesterday. G. Minott says that he saw some a week ago.

June 13, 1854

I find them [arrowheads] on all sides—not only in corn and grain and potato and bean fields—but in pastures and woods—by woodchucks' holes—and pigeon beds—and as tonight in a pasture where a restless cow had pawed the ground.

July 18, 1854

Brooks has let out some of his pigeons which stay about the stands or perches to bait others. Wild ones nest in his woods quite often. He begins to catch them the middle of August.

August 15, 1854

Crossed from top of Annursnack to top of Strawberry Hill—past a pigeon bed. . . .

In the meanwhile we came upon another pigeon bed where the pigeons were being baited—a little corn etc. being spread on the ground—and at the first the bower was already erected.

August 16, 1854

Says [John Russell] that in Chelmsford they rub the pigeon bait with the *S. odora* [sweet goldenrod] to attract pigeons.

August 26, 1854

Pigeons with their *quivet* dashed over the Dugan Desert.

August 27, 1854

Many red oak acorns have fallen. The great green acorns in broad shallow cups. How attractive these forms! No wonder they are imitated on pumps—fence—and bed posts. Is not this a reason that the pigeons are about? . . . As I go up Pine Hill, gather the shriveled *V. vacillans* berries [hillside blueberries]—many as hard as if dried on a pan. They are very sweet and good and not wormy like the huckleberries. Far more abundant in this state than usual owing to the drought. As I stand there I think I hear a rising wind rustling the tops of the woods—and turning see what I think is the rear of a large flock of pigeons. Do they not eat many of these berries?...

[N]ow reaching on higher land some open pigeon place—a breathing place for us.

September 5, 1854

Barrett shows me some very handsome pear-shaped cranberries not uncommon which may be a permanent variety different from the common rounded ones. Saw two pigeons which flew about his pond and then lit on the elms over his house—he said they had come to drink from Brooks' as they often did. He sees a blue heron there almost every morning of late. Such is the place for them.

September 8, 1854

He [Garfield] heard some years ago a large flock of brant go over—"yelling" very loud, flying low and in an irregular dense flock like pigeons.

September 10, 1854

Have seen pigeons about a fortnight.

September 12, 1854

I scare pigeons from Hubbard's oaks beyond. How like the creaking of trees the slight sounds they make! Thus they are concealed. Not only their *prating* or *quivet* is like a sharp creak—but I heard a sound from them like a dull grating or cracking of bough on bough....

On a white oak beyond Everett's orchard by the road I see quite a flock of pigeons and their blue black droppings and their feathers spot the road. The bare limbs of the oak apparently attracted them—though its acorns are thick on the ground. These are found whole in their crops. They swallow them whole. I should think from the droppings that they had been eating berries. I hear that Wetherbee caught 92 dozen last week.

September 16, 1854

One man thinks there are not so many pigeons as last week—that it is too cold for them. . . . I see little flocks of chip-birds along the roadside and on the apple trees showing their light undersides when they rise.

December 8, 1854

There is a glorious clear sunset sky—soft and delicate and warm even like a pigeon's neck. Why do the mountains never look so fair as from my native fields?

January 24, 1855

I am [reading] William Wood's "New England's Prospect." He left New England August 15th, 1633—and the last English edition referred to in this American one of 1764 is that of London 1639. . . .

Eagles are probably less common. Pigeons of course *vide* Indian book—heath cocks all gone, price "4 pence"—and turkeys, good cock, "4 shillings". . . .

Of pigeons "Many of them build amongst the Pine-trees, thirty miles to the North-east of our plantations; joyning nest to nest, and tree to tree by their nests, so that the Sunne never sees the ground in that place, from whence the *Indians* fetch whole loades of them."

April 16, 1855

In the meanwhile heard the *quivet* through the wood—and looking saw through an opening a small compact flock of pigeons flying low about. . . . Now and then they [sheldrakes] seemed to see or hear or smell us—and uttered a low note of alarm—something like the note of a tree toad, but very faint—or perhaps a little more wiry and like that of pigeons—but the sleepers hardly lifted their heads for it.

April 26, 1855

Going over Ponkawtasset—hear a golden-crested (?) wren—the robin's note etc.—in the tops of the high wood—see myrtle birds—and half a dozen pigeons. The *prate* of the last is much like the creaking of a tree. They lift their wings at the same moment as they sit. There are said to be many about now. See their warm colored breasts.

April 27, 1855

Heard a singular sort of screech somewhat like a hawk under the Cliff—and soon some pigeons flew out of a pine near me.

May 26, 1855

See a beautiful blue-backed and long-tailed pigeon sitting daintily on a low white pine limb.

August 29, 1855

Saw two green-winged teal—somewhat pigeon-like on a flat low rock in the Assabet.

April 17, 1856

I love to hear the voice of the first thunder—as of the toad (though it returns irregularly like pigeons) far away in *his* moist meadow—where he is warmed to life—and see the flash of his eye.

April 22, 1856

By the path and in the sandy field beyond are many of those star-fingered puffballs. I think they must be those which are so white like pigeons' eggs in the fall—the thick leathery rind bursting into 8 to 11 segments like those of a boy's batting ball and curving back.

June 30, 1856

Borrowed Roberts' boat—shaped like a pumpkin seed—for he wished to paddle on Great Quittacas. Roberts is the mean Calvinist minister from England a dozen or more years since. Ricketson was invited to dine there once. There was a great parade and all the *forms* of hospitality—but the chief food was one pigeon—all of which was eaten by the son.

September 2, 1856

A few pigeons were seen a fortnight ago. I have noticed none in all walks—but G. Minott—whose mind runs on them so much—but whose age and infirmities confine him to his woodshed on the hillside saw a small flock a fortnight ago. I rarely pass at any season of the year but he asks if I have seen any pigeons. One man's mind running on pigeons will sit thus in the midst of a village—many of whose inhabitants never see nor dream of a pigeon except in the pot—and where even naturalists do not observe—and he looking out with expectation and faith from morning till night—will surely see them.

September 16, 1856

See a flock of pigeons dash by—from a stout breast they taper straightly and slenderly to the tail. They have been catching them a while.

February 4, 1857

Told [Minott] a story about one Josh Piper, a harelipped man—who lived down east awhile—whose wife would not let him occupy her bed—but he used to catch ducks there in a net on the shore as they do pigeons—and so got feathers enough to fill the bed—and therefore thought he had a right to be on it.

April 11, 1857

The very fishes in countless schools are driven out of a river by the *improvements* of the civilized man—as the pigeon and other fowls out of the air.

May 14, 1857

Abel Hosmer tells me that he has collected and sown white pine seed—and that he has found them in the crop of pigeons. (?)

September 27, 1857

Many birds are common to the northern parts of both continents [Europe and North America]. Even the passenger pigeon has flown across there.

September 30, 1857

Minott said he had seen a couple of pigeons go over at last—as he sat in his shed. At first he thought they were doves but he soon saw that they were pigeons they flew so straight and fast.

May 19, 1858

Looking with my glass into the Gourgas pond hole—and see *three* or *four* buckbean blossoms. Two birds about the size and of the appearance of a pigeon or turtle dove start up with a loud alarm note from the shallow muddy flat there—with a harsh shrill cry—*whil whil whil* or the like. At first I could not guess what they were, but since conclude that they were the large yellow-legs.

June 2, 1858

We met a man (apparently an Indian or Canadian half breed) and a boy with guns who had been out after pigeons but only killed five crows.

August 17, 1858

C. saw pigeons today.

September 9, 1858

R. [Israel Rice] says that he has caught pigeons which had ripe grapes in their crops long before any were ripe here—and that they came from the southwest.

September 13, 1858

A small dense flock of wild pigeons dashes by over the side of the hill from west to east—perhaps from Wetherbee's to Brooks'—for I see the latter's pigeon place. They make a dark-slate gray impression.

September 23, 1858

Met a gunner from Lynn on the beach [Rockport] who had several pigeons which he had killed in the woods by the shore. Said they had been blown off the mainland.

March 19, 1859

Melvin says that in skinning a mink you must cut round the parts containing the musk—else the operation will be an offensive one—that Wetherbee has already baited some pigeons (he hears)—that he last year found a hen hawk's eggs in March—and thinks that woodcocks are now laying.

April 12, 1859

Pine warblers heard in the woods by C. today. This except the pigeon woodpecker and pigeon and hawks as far as they are migratory—is the first that I should call woodland (or dry woodland) birds that arrives.

April 18, 1859

I am looking for acorns these days, to sow on the Walden lot but can find very few sound ones. Those which the squirrels have not got are mostly worm eaten and quite pulverized or decayed. A few—which are cracked at the small, having started last fall, have yet life in them—perhaps enough to plant. Even these look rather discolored when you cut them open, but Buttrick says they will do for pigeon bait—so each man looks at things from his own point of view.

May 7, 1859

I frequently see pigeons dashing about in small flocks or three or four at a time over the woods here [Acton]. Theirs is a peculiarly swift dashing flight.

September 1, 1859

If you would study the birds now—go where their food is—i.e. the berries—especially to the wild black cherries—elderberries—pokeberries—mountain ash berries—and ere long the barberries—and for pigeons the acorns.

September 9, 1859

I start many pigeons now in a sproutland.

September 13, 1859

It is a wonder how pigeons can swallow acorns whole, but they do.

September 14, 1859

They are catching pigeons nowadays. Coombs has a stand west of Nut Meadow—and he says that he has just shot 14 hawks there which were after the pigeons. I have one which he has shot within a day or two—and calls a pigeon hawk.

September 15, 1859

Dense flocks of pigeons fly hurry skurry over the hill. Pass near Brooks' pigeon stands. There was a flock perched on his poles—and they sat so still and in such regular order there, being also the color of the wood, that I thought they were wooden figures at first. They were perched not only in horizontal straight lines one above the other—which the cross bars required—but at equal distances apart on these perches, which must be their own habit—and it struck me that they made just such a figure seen against the sky—as pigeon holes cut in a dove's house do (i.e. a more or less triangular figure thus) and possibly the seeing them such perched might have originally suggested this arrangement of the holes.

Pigeons dart by on every side—a dry slate color, like weather stained wood (the weather stained birds) fit color for this aerial traveler—a more subdued and earthy blue than the sky—as its field (or path) is between the sky and the earth. Not black or brown, as is the earth—but a terrene or slaty blue suggesting their aerial resorts and habits.

September 21, 1859

I sat near Coombs' pigeon place by White Pond. The pigeons sat motionless on his bare perches—from time to time dropping down into the bed—and uttering a *quivet* or two. Some stood on the perch—others squatted flat. I could see their dove-colored breasts. Then all at once, being alarmed, would take to flight but ere long return in straggling parties.

He tells me that he has 15 dozen baited—but does not intend to catch any more at present or for two or three weeks—hoping to attract others. Rice says that white oak acorns pounded up shells and all make the best bait for them.

September 26, 1859

Hearing a sharp *phe-phe* and again—*phe-phe-phe* I look round and see two (probably larger) yellow-legs like pigeons standing in the water by the bare flat ammannia [redstem] shore—their whole forms reflected in the water. They allow me to paddle past them though on the alert.

September 28, 1859

The white pine seed is very abundant this year and this must attract more pigeons. Coombs tells me that he finds the seed in their crops. Also that he found within a day or two a full formed egg with shell in one.

October 2, 1859

As I sat on an old pigeon stand, not used this year on the hill south of the swamp—at the foot of a tree set up with perches nailed on it—a pigeon hawk, as I take it, came and perched on the tree. As if it had been wont to catch pigeons at such places.

November 8, 1859

Coombs says that quite a little flock of pigeons bred here last summer. He found one nest in a small white pine near his pigeon stand (where he baited them in the summer) so low he could put his hand in it!?

January 23, 1860

Minott says that pigeons alight in great flocks on the tops of hemlocks in March, and he thinks they eat the seed. (But he also thought for the same reason that they ate the white pine seed at the same season—when it is not there! They might find a little of the last adhering to the pitch.)

June 2, 1860

Saw a pigeon yesterday—a turtle dove today.

June 14, 1860

See a pigeon.

September 4, 1860

Saw flocks of pigeons the 2d and 3d. I see and hear on Conantum an upland plover. The goldfinch is very busy pulling the thistle to pieces.

October 8, 1860

Standing by a pigeon place on the north edge Damon's lot—I saw on the dead top of a white pine four or five rods off—which had been stripped for 15 feet downward that it might die and afford with its branches a perch for the pigeons about the place—like the more artificial ones that were set up—two woodpeckers that were new to me.

October 19, 1860

It is a remarkable fact—and looks like a glaring imperfection in Nature—that the labor of the oaks for the year should be lost to this extent. The softening or freezing of cranberries—the rotting of potatoes—etc. etc. seem trifling in comparison. The pigeons jays squirrels—and woodlands are thus impoverished. It is hard to say what great purpose is served by this seeming waste.

November 2, 1860

Wetherbee's oak lot may contain four or five acres. He says eight. The trees are white, red, scarlet—and swamp white oaks—maple—white pine and ash. They are unusually large and old. Indeed I doubt if there is another hereabouts of oaks as large. It is said that Wetherbee left them for the sake of mast for pigeons.

November 10, 1860

This wood [Inches Wood] is said to have been a great resort for pigeons. We saw one large pigeon place—on the top of the hill where we first entered it. Now used.

THE NIGHT WARBLER

APPENDIX B

Despite the disparaging remarks about Thoreau's ability as a birder, the editors of the 1906 edition admit that "bird-loving readers" might find the Journal to be "a desirable store of ornithological nuts to crack on winter evenings."

> Some such reader, by a careful collation of the data which the publication of the journal as a whole puts at his disposal, will perhaps succeed in settling the identity of the famous "night-warbler;" a bird which some, we believe, have suspected to be nothing rarer than the almost superabundant ovenbird, but which, so far as we ourselves know, may have been almost any one (or any two or three) of our smaller common birds that are given to occasional ecstatic song-flights. Whatever it was, it was of use to Thoreau for the quickening of his imagination, and for literary purposes; and Emerson was well advised in warning him to beware of booking it, lest life henceforth should have so much the less to show him.

The identity of the night warbler was a nut that Thoreau himself never cracked. In "The Allegash and East Branch," published in *The Maine Woods* after his death, Thoreau relates his third expedition to Maine in 1857. On July 26, he camped with Joe Polis on the Caucomgomoc River, about ten miles from Caucomgomoc Lake. "I heard a night-warbler, wood thrush, kingfisher, tweezer bird or particolored warbler, and a nighthawk."

June 11, 1851

I hear the night singing bird breaking out as in his dreams, made so from the first for some mysterious reason.

June 29, 1851

The night warbler sings the same strain at noon.

February 3, 1852

That little bird that I hear and call the night warbler—may be translated *Noctu suave canens* [singing sweetly at night].

May 8, 1852

The song sparrow and the robin sing early and late. The night warbler while it is yet pretty light.

May 9, 1852

Heard the night warbler.

May 14, 1852

Hear the robin—ovenbird—night warbler—and at length the towhee's *towee*—chickadee's *phebe*—and a preluding thrasher—and a jay.

June 15, 1852

Quite a feast of strawberries on Fair Haven, the upland strawberry. The largest and sweetest on sand. The *first fruit*. The night warbler.

August 17, 1852

The woods are very still. I hear only a faint peep or twitter from one bird—then the never-failing wood thrush—it being about sunrise and after on the Cliff—the *phebe* note of a chickadee—a night warbler—a creeper? and a pewee?—and later still the huckleberry bird and red-eye—but all few and faint.

April 8, 1853

Is not my night warbler the white-eyed vireo? Not yet here. Heard the field sparrow again.

May 9, 1853

Again I think I heard the night warbler. Now at starlight that same night hawk or snipe squeak is heard—but no hovering.

May 10, 1853

Hear the night warbler now distinctly. It does not soon repeat its note—and disappears with the sound.

June 18, 1853

The night warbler—and again afterward.

It is worth the while to walk thus in the night after a warm or sultry day to enjoy the fresh up-country—brake-like—springlike scent in low grounds.

June 19, 1853

Heard my night warbler on a solitary white pine in the Heywood Clearing by the Peak. Discovered it at last looking like a small piece of black bark curving partly over the limb. No fork to its tail. It appeared black beneath—was very shy—not bigger than a yellowbird and more slender.

May 10, 1854

Heard the first regular bullfrog trump—not *very* loud however—at the swamp. White oaks southwest of Pantry. Heard the night warbler.

May 28, 1854

The night warbler after his strain drops down almost perpendicularly into a treetop and is lost.

May 29, 1854

Saw what I thought my night warbler, sparrow-like with chestnut (?) stripes on breast, white or whitish below and about eyes—and perhaps chestnut (??) head.

July 10, 1854

Night warbler of late.

July 18, 1854

I think I have not heard a night warbler for a fortnight.

July 28, 1854

Night warbler and evergreen forest note not lately.

August 12, 1854

No night warbler, hear one at evening August 14—or tweezer—or evergreen forest note—nor veery.

May 12, 1855

The brown thrasher is a powerful singer—he is a quarter of a mile off across the river, when he sounded within 15 rods.

Hear the night warbler....

Just before sundown took our seats before the owl's nest and sat perfectly still and awaited her appearance. We sat about half an hour—and it was surprising what various distinct sounds we heard there deep in the wood—as if the aisles of the wood were so many ear trumpets—the cawing of crows—the peeping of hylas [spring peepers] in the swamp—and perhaps the croaking of a tree toad—the ovenbird—the *yorrick* of Wilson's thrush [veery]—a distant stake driver—the night warbler—and black and white creeper—the lowing of cows—the late supper horn—the voices of boys—the singing of girls—not all together but separately and distinctly and musically from where the partridge—and the red-tailed hawk and the screech owl sit on their nests.

May 13, 1855

At 9.30 P.M. I hear from our gate—my night warbler. Never heard it in the village before.

May 15, 1856

On *Amelanchier Botryapium* [smooth shadbush] many narrow dark bronze-colored beetles (say ¾ inch long) coupled and at same time eating the flowers calyx and all.

Night warbler.

May 3, 1857

Emerson says that Brewer tells him my "night warbler" is probably the Nashville warbler.

May 12, 1857

A night warbler—plainly light beneath. It always flies to a new perch immediately after its song.

January 15, 1858

Speaking to him [Dr. Kneeland] of my night warbler he asked if it uttered such a note—making the note of the myrtle bird, *ah, tetete tetete tetete* exactly, and said that that was the note of the white-throated sparrow—which he heard at Lake Superior (at night as well as by day).

May 16, 1858

A golden-crowned thrush hops quite near. It is quite small about the size of the creeper—with the upper part of its breast thickly and distinctly penciled with black—a tawny head and utters *now* only a sharp cluck for a *chirp*.

See and hear a redstart, the rhythm of whose strain is *tse\tse, tse\tse, tse*—emphasizing the last syllable of all—and not ending with the common *tsear*. Hear the night warbler.

May 17, 1858

Just after hearing my night warbler—I see two birds on a tree. The one which I examined, as well as I could without a glass, had a white throat with a white spot on his wings—was dark above and moved from time to time like a creeper—and it was about the creeper's size. The other bird which I did not examine particularly was a little larger and more tawny—perhaps golden-crowned thrush.

May 19, 1858

Heard the night warbler—begin his strain just like an ovenbird! I have noticed that when it drops down into the woods—it darts suddenly *one side* to a perch when low.

June 19, 1858

I do not hear this night warbler so often as a few weeks ago. Birds generally do not sing so tumultuously.

July 6, 1858

We see the handsome *Malva sylvestris* [high mallow] (an introduced flower) by roadside, apparently in prime and also in Conway [New Hampshire]—and hear the night warbler all along thus far.

August 5, 1858

Fair Haven Pond. While passing there, I heard *what I should call* my night warbler's note—and looking up saw the bird dropping to a bush on the hillside. Looking through the glass I saw that it was the Maryland yellow-throat!! And it afterward flew to the buttonbushes in the meadow.

May 13, 1859

Surveying Damon's Acton lot.

Hear the *pe-pe* and evergreen forest note—also night warbler (the last perhaps the 11th).

May 8, 1860

A cloudy day.

The small pewee how long. The night warbler's note. River 4⅞ inches below summer level. Stone-heaps, how long?

May 18, 1860

The night warbler is a *powerful* singer for so small a bird. It launches into the air above the forest—or over some hollow or open space in the woods—and challenges the attention of the woods by its rapid and impetuous warble and then drops down swiftly into the treetops like a performer withdrawing behind the scenes—and he is very lucky who detects where it alights.

August 28, 1860

Hear the night warbler and the whippoorwill.

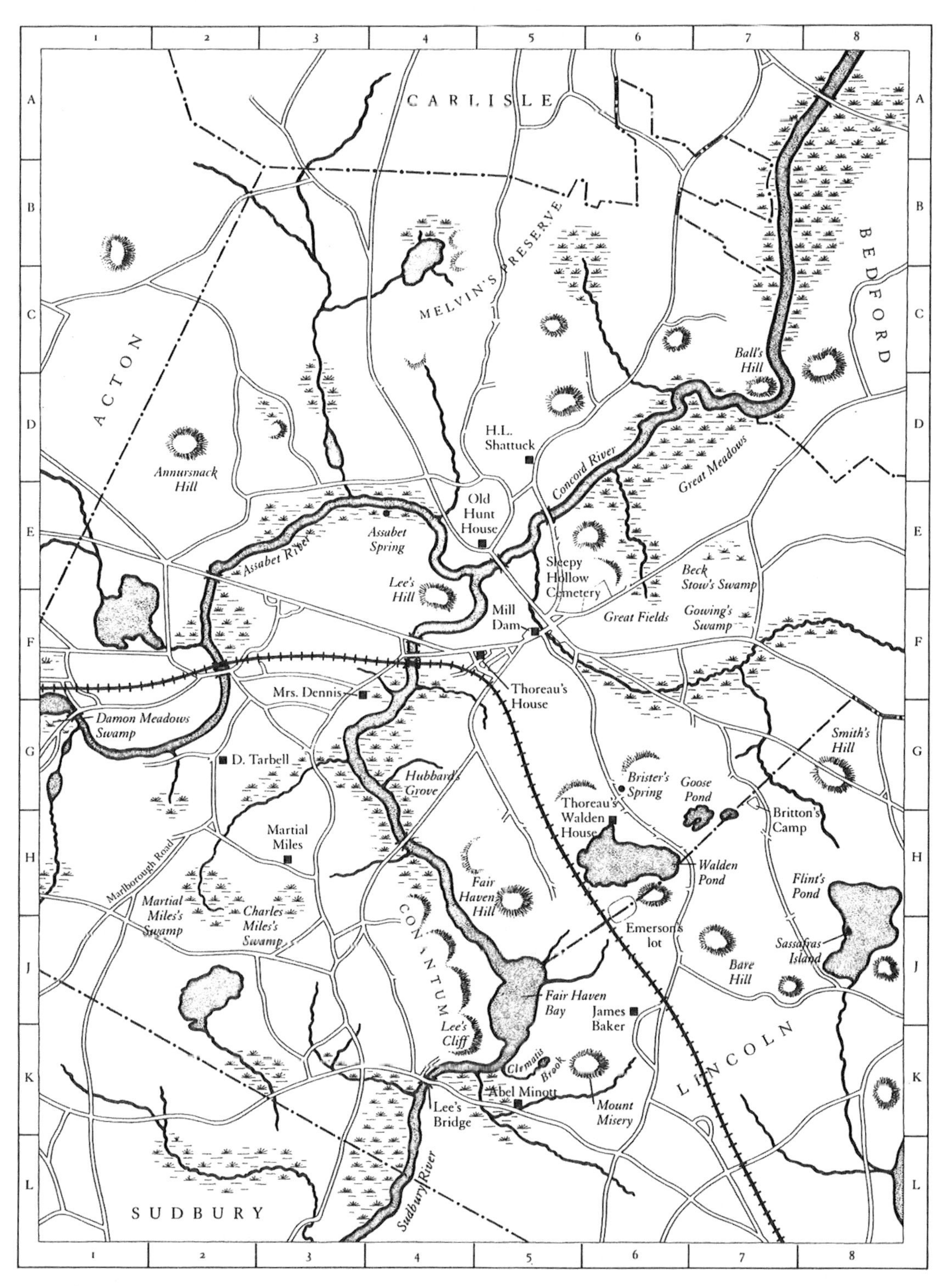

Concord, Massachusetts, based on a map compiled by Herbert W. Gleason in 1906. (From *Faith in a Seed*, by Henry D. Thoreau. Copyright 1993 by Island Press. Reproduced by permission of Island Press, Washington, DC.)

BIBLIOGRAPHY

Alden, Peter and Brian Cassie. *National Audubon Society Field Guide to New England*. New York: Knopf, 1998.

Angelo, Ray. *Thoreau Place Names: A Guide to Place Names in Concord and Lincoln, MA in the Journal of Henry David Thoreau*. https://archive.org/details/thoreau-place-names/.

Arsić, Branka. *Bird Relics: Grief and Vitalism in Thoreau*. Cambridge, MA: Harvard University Press, 2016.

Audubon, John James. *Birds of America*. New York and London: Prestel, 2021.

Bosco, Ronald A., ed. *Nature's Panorama: Thoreau on the Seasons*. Amherst and Boston: University of Massachusetts Press, 2005.

Cruickshank, Helen, ed. *Thoreau on Birds*. New York: McGraw-Hill, 1964.

Grant, Steve, ed. *Daily Observations: Thoreau on the Days of the Year*. Amherst and Boston: University of Massachusetts Press, 2005.

Griscom, Ludlow. *Birds of Concord*. Cambridge, MA: Harvard University Press, 1949.

Howarth, William. *The Book of Concord: Thoreau's Life as a Writer*. New York: Penguin, 1983.

Miller, Perry. *Consciousness in Concord: The Text of Thoreau's Hitherto Lost Journal (1840–1841) Together with Notes and a Commentary*. Boston: Houghton Mifflin, 1958.

Nilsson, Lennart, ed. *Henry David Thoreau: Fågeldagbok* [Bird Diary]. Malmö, Sweden: Ellerströms, 2009.

Richardson Jr., Robert D. *Henry Thoreau: A Life of the Mind*. Oakland: University of California Press, 1986.

Schorger, A.W. *The Passenger Pigeon: Its Natural History and Extinction*. Caldwell, NJ: Blackburn Press, 1955.

Thoreau, Henry David. *The Journal of Henry D. Thoreau*. Edited by Bradford Torrey and Francis H. Allen. New York: Dover, 1962. Reprint of 1906 edition.

———. *Thoreau's Notes on Birds of New England*. Edited by Francis H. Allen. Mineola, NY: Dover, 2019. Reprint of 1910 edition.

———. *The Writings of Henry David Thoreau: Journal, Volumes 1–8*. Princeton, NJ: Princeton University Press, 1981–2002.

INDEX